Noses in the Wind:

How to Create the Best Life for Your Dog (and Make a Forever Home)

Lisa Andrea Snyder

Strategic Book Publishing and Rights Co.

Strategic Book Publishing and Rights Co., LLC
USA
www.sbpra.net

For information about special discounts for bulk purchases, please contact Strategic Book Publishing and Rights Co. Special Sales, at bookorder@sbpra.net.

ISBN: 978-1-68235-717-0

Book Design: Suzanne Kelly

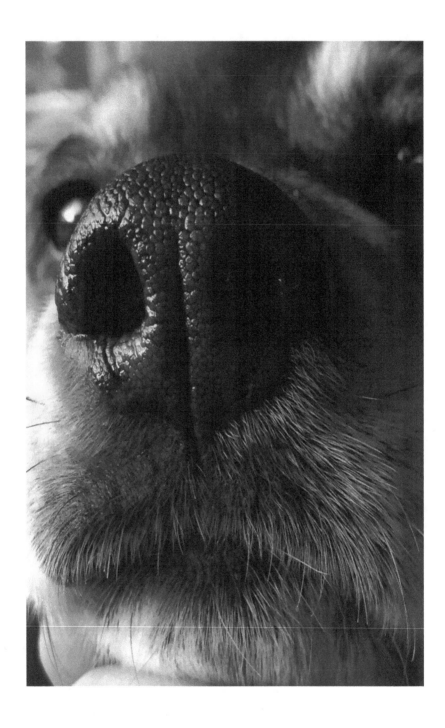

The Dog's Nose

Dogs can smell forty feet under the ground
Small dogs, medium dogs, and the giant hound.
Sniffing out cancer cells or an impeding health event
They can identify other species by pheromone scent.
Smelling in 3-D because each nostril works alone
It really is amazing, so just *try* to hide that bone.
They rely on their noses completely; it's how they figure
    everything out
Smelling a hundred thousand times better than we can with
    our human snout.
Sniffing can be as important as physical exercise
It's their largest agency, their biggest enterprise.
So when you take them out, let them sniff to their heart's
    delight
Show respect for dogs' noses as they really are their sight.
Please don't pull or drag them, just let them find their pace
And you will learn more patience, bearing witness to dogs'
    grace.

— *Lisa Andrea Snyder*

Foreword

THANK YOU SO MUCH FOR choosing to read this book on how to create *the absolute best life for your dog.*

It is an honor to have had so much joy with dogs in my life, and I know I would not be the human I am today, nor had half the joy, without these sentient creatures surrounding me.

The concepts and suggestions outlined in this book are all basic. If you are a dog lover and have been for decades, perhaps not all this information is news to you, but you just may enjoy it anyway. If you don't have a dog yet but want one, or are not sure if you should get a dog because of your busy life, read on. This book is absolutely for you!

The recognition that your lifestyle/household may not be able to accommodate having a dog is what's fair, mature, and honorable. What is not fair, mature, or honorable is getting a dog, a sentient creature full of feelings and needs, and not mapping out a plan whatsoever for their daily exercise and mental stimulation. These are great concerns to be heavily weighed that I humorously, and at times quite seriously, address.

I just wanted to introduce myself to you and to convey that dogs really help us to live our lives with greater purpose. They really improve the lives of individuals and families, and the ensuing joy is worth the work, but you must know that it *is* work.

So, thank you for taking your time to buy and read this book during your busy life.

It *all* came from my heart and a whole lot of true love, respect, and admiration for the dog.

Cheers to the dog!

Table of Contents

CHAPTER 1

Who Am I, and Why Should You Listen to Anything I Say?

WHEN THE RECESSION OF 2007–2010 HAPPENED, I watched my short-lived real estate career start to take a nosedive. I had just purchased a new home and my career was really starting to take off. Yep, just as it looked like I had finally found the perfect career, this is when the economy completely tanked—a.k.a. the mortgage crisis.

With my own new mortgage and a decent amount of debt, I had to think of a career that could support my financial nut every month *and* simultaneously be something that I could love. I had been unconventional in most aspects of my life, so I already knew that getting just any job would not suffice. I was lucky enough to have had jobs over the years that supported me that I liked a lot, and was even successful in (mostly sales), but to have to recreate yourself in your mid-forties was especially anxiety-producing, because I didn't really fit into any career box.

In addition, I had never married or had children, so it was just me—good in some ways, lonely and scary in others.

When I was speaking to a wise friend of mine, she said four very simple words: "Do what
you love."
I said, "Really? Come on. Isn't that a tad simplistic?"
She then repeated, "Do what you love."
I mean, doesn't everyone want to earn their living by doing what they love? We were not all born artists or trust fund babies.

1

I believe that most people are not so sure what their future holds for them, as compared to some annoyingly together friends who say things like "I knew I wanted to be a doctor when I was four." I mean, maybe, but certainly not for the majority of us. The reality is that most of us get on the job and career trains right out of high school, or the trade path, or after four or six years of college and get into *life*.

As we all know by now, life goes fast and, *poof,* you are pushing forty before you know it. It just happens—and it happened to me. I was basically a woman doing her thing, and the recession happened to throw me a very scary and specific curveball.

"So, what now, girl? How will you make your money? Oh, no! How will I pay for health insurance and dog food—and dog food is *not* cheap, because I make it, and I have always had between one and four dogs."

On and on my head spun, and it did so relentlessly. I urged myself to calm down, to think about what it was *precisely* that I loved. As one of millions of people who suffer from extreme anxiety, I really needed a plan. The real estate deals were done. I had enough money for a few months, but I felt the panic coming.

Do what you love.

Do what you love.

Well, I love dogs! I do. I love people and cats and horses, and I am pretty sure I could love a goat, a monkey, and a pangolin. Simply put, I love animals! Mostly, though, I love dogs.

I got my first dog when I was twenty-six. Losing Mr. Bogie twelve years later was the first huge loss I had ever experienced as a human being. When he died, I was so emotionally overwrought that I could not get another dog for seven years (a common story, and I address this in Chapter 20). Anyway, I literally could not bring up Bogie's name without tearing up for close to two decades.

Evidently, that is how I love—deeply and intensely. Perhaps it's just too much love, if there is such a thing.

I am in utter awe of every dog I have ever had. I could barely wait to get home to see them, love them, care for them. *Never* were they a burden (until it was time to travel, and the chapter on boarding them addresses this).

Anyway, I love all dogs, from fancy to thug! I have never met a dog I couldn't love, and I eventually moved along to helping find homes for strays. In 2016, I launched my website called The Canine American (www.thecanineamerican.com) to help support organizations that are trying to end the dog meat trade in Asia.

So, I started a dog-walking business. My hope was to make an extra $500 or so per month while doing something else that I would deem the "real" job. The money I made dog walking was merely to subsidize the extras in my life, but what happened was the following:

I began with an article in a local hometown magazine. I called my venture Dog Day Afternoon and registered as a local business. Dog Day Afternoon commenced in September 2010 and within one year provided me with *all* the necessary income by doing what I love. OMG! Astounding! Of course, there's never enough money in one's mind, so I continued to grow Dog Day Afternoon. That one article introduced the "dogs gone wild" and freedom concept while conveying my crazy love of dogs—photos and everything.

My customer base grew quickly, and then came the referrals. The concept was unusual, and it *really* took off in the small funky village of Nyack on the Hudson, New York, and its surrounding towns.

It was a variation on the theme of dog walking—with *no* leashes. Twice a day, I took two different groups of dogs—two PACs (playfully active canines)—out into the woods. Rockland County, New York, has so many beautiful areas and state parks, which I shall not name, because currently there are other PAC leaders taking dogs on adventures, and out of respect, I wish to preserve their businesses and their ability to make a living.

The point is that within one year I had enough customers to pay my mortgage and bills *and* save $250 a month. It was far from what I considered "set," and not as much as I had earned in real estate, but the hours suited me immensely, as did not working on the weekends!

Running a group of seven to ten dogs in the woods requires skill, and boy, was that one steep learning curve! I had to learn one day at a time and simply put to honor my vision. In the woods, one must be ready for anything, from snake encounters to crazy high-speed deer chases to a possible hurt paw that automatically comes with the possibility of carrying a dog out of the woods. (That never happened but it could have.)

All the PAC members must be licensed, vaccinated, and kind. There are rules for state-run land (as this world is just full of rules, rules, and more rules), so I had to learn to steer around them—or run, literally, in some cases.

Regular issues included running into a person who had their dog leashed in these remote areas who was a tad startled by having PAC members approach quickly and all at once. *Usually,* they then let their dog off leash and just watched with awe as their dog quickly matriculated in with the free bunch, bearing witness to the ultra play and exercise that always naturally ensued. Occasionally, people showed fear or even reprimanded me for this non-conformist style of exercising dogs. Over the years of running into those same dog people (sometimes daily), I not only lost their admonishment, but I gained their respect, and several even became clients.

Naturally, there were always a few that had to yell at me (there is always that one person, right?). They would try to convince me that their dog was vicious and to stay back. This person almost always had a sweet-looking dog just yearning to join in on the fun, but this type of person doesn't permit their dog to socialize—probably due to fear (perhaps they had witnessed a prior dog attack)—so now their poor dog is forbidden to play. Their dog usually sits calmly wagging its beautiful tail. To be fair, some dogs are unfriendly and on a leash for various reasons, but sometimes even these people and their dogs got used to seeing us, ultimately just ignoring us. Most waved.

Honestly, my PAC was so well trained with mere voice control that they would abide a command and completely ignore the person I just described. People started asking me if I could train their dog. I then told them what I am telling you here:

1. My only credential was the sheer freedom I offered dogs, as I have no formal training.

2. Most dogs, if respected enough to be exercised properly and plentifully and have adequate focus and energy bestowed upon them, do not need any formal training.

You see, when a dog experiences the ability to be and enjoy who and what they are (wild animals with wild spirits), when they can socialize with other dogs who become friends over time (social pack animals), when they are not forced to sit with their pee and poop for too many hours and/or forced to be bored to death; when they are *truly* a part of you or your families' lives and not just a burden; *when our dogs are fully acknowledged and respected for who and what they are*, they live their best lives!

A dog living its best life = A happy dog = No destructive behavior

Truthfully, if you cannot give these basics to a dog, you probably should not have one (sorry, this must be said). Dogs will understand what you want from them through the vessels of time and repetition. Using a sound and resolute command, communication between a person and their dog may eventually feel telepathic. While I could have gotten trainer credentialed, I felt qualified to change a dog's life by simply understanding them. All I was in fact was a facilitator, a conduit to freedom and joy.

For eight years, I facilitated dog freedom and enjoyed the utter rapture of bearing witness to complete dog joy. I became known as "the dog lady." I got so much exercise that I ended up with bone spurs on the top parts of both feet, but I felt consumed with joy regarding this career choice.

Of course, there were a few incidents over that span of time (rarely), but things happen. A dog would disappear but would inevitably meet me at my truck when they were done with their total freedom romp. Mind you, we were in the deep woods, nowhere near any roads. Nerve-racking, but it proved to be one of the most important lessons: *They always come back!*

I trained myself to stop panicking and to trust. This saved me a *lot* of stress. Usually, it was just one predictable dog named Molly (a hound) that had the urge to chase, but learning not to worry or panic when a dog ran off was key, as their superior radar system far outsmarts ours. When in the woods that beginning year, it was the individual radar of each PAC member that I came to rely on—my point being that while we absolutely freak out because our dog has bolted, trust me, *please,* when I tell you that they are literally tracking you. If chasing deer (by the way, that's as good as it gets for a dog), even if they end up miles out, they always ended up back in the PAC by the end of the "adventure" or back at my truck. This was a massive lesson. Impeccable timing, all in all, and in eight years, what I just described happened only a handful of times.

There is absolutely no reason your dog, the love of your life, must be attached to a leash for every single outing. If you want to increase their happiness and their joy, figure this bit out. Find a place to let them romp free off the leash—literally the chain that binds them. Throw a little caution to the wind to find out that your dog will not run away from you (as most people falsely assume), and begin to assert control with your voice. You will see a *huge* difference in your creature when they are getting their dog on. Doggone it!

I am not saying that some dogs won't experiment with their newfound freedom. *They most certainly will.* Just keep walking and have trust that they will follow in the general direction, and get used to this. Learn how to navigate, as this is new for the both of you.

Fear and mistrust have kept dogs bound their entire lives. Perhaps you live near a beach or a huge ballfield that is not always in use, or a trail on which you have seen loose dogs. EXPERIMENT!

Winters in the Northeast can be challenging (okay, brutal), and while most people were cozy at home or in their offices, I was out all day long transporting and facilitating *joy for dogs*. It was a glorious time. I earned good money for no more than five or six hours a day, and I felt I was doing an incredible service for those lucky dogs. My only wish was that all dogs could experience this type of natural freedom in giant yards, ballfields, and in the woods.

So, this is who I am. This is who is dispensing advice from this little book.

I want to convey as much as I can from what I learned during this time. I did *not* expect this career to last almost a decade. I thought for sure it was going to be temporary, but what I witnessed daily satisfied something deep in my soul. I felt that I was on to something, and I was. I am a woman who still hikes her own dogs off leash twice daily, and a woman who wants to help you understand how dogs thrive if given the opportunity to.

- A happy, satisfied dog will not be a destructive dog.
- A happy, satisfied dog will be a healthier dog (physically and emotionally).
- Therefore, he or she will not be returned to the shelter, pound, or breeder.
- A happy, satisfied dog will be permanently homed.

This is what I aspire to—assisting dogs in being permanently homed! So, please read on in the best of health!

Write to me at lisa@thecanineamerican.com if you have any questions, and I welcome your feedback.

Namaste, or Doggiestay!

CHAPTER 2

Who is a Dog Person?

THERE ARE DOG PEOPLE AND then there are *dog people*, but you do *not* have to be the Dog Whisperer to have a dog. You just must be a good person and have the desire for this type of loyal and gorgeous companionship.

This bond is not to be taken lightly or halfheartedly. Dogs love us and our families like you cannot believe. Some dogs have a bad history, but even the damaged and the traumatized have a great propensity to love and be loved. We, the humans, must know this and act accordingly. Some of you more rural readers may want a backyard dog on the property for protection more than for companionship. You feed them and care for them, but perhaps you don't really connect. Even this old school "yard dog" relationship can be tweaked, yielding a more rewarding and happy relationship for both. It just takes awareness.

Consciousness is at the Root of Everything

Some parents get dogs simply because it's 2022 and kids rule, so if your little prince or princess says, "Daddy/Mommy, I want a dog!", you heed this request because God forbid your kids don't have what the neighbors have or their best friends have. You embark on your quest for a Lab or a Golden because you heard they were the perfect family dog, or a Doodle because when your allergy-riddled mother or in-law comes to visit, they may be impacted. So, you pony up the $3,000 (plus) and get yourself a Doodle (which, unless third generation, is not a full-on, allergy-free dog!).

The dogs I just mentioned are great dogs, because . . . *all dogs are great!* Breeds, mutts, rescues = great. This is the God's honest truth.

You may love Collies because you had one as a child, so you are going to want a Collie. You heard German Shepherds are super intelligent and great guard dogs. You are right, but you are still describing almost every single dog out there. You want a dog you can run with that is super Type A and high energy like yourself. You heard a Border Collie or a hound loves running, and the truth is that all dogs would love to go for a run. The bigger truth is that if you are running (especially in hot weather and more than one mile—and you probably are) it is *awful* to be a dog. Your dog will follow because they are not given a choice, but it is cruel. It is much easier to run *free* and unrestrained. So do that. Run free and unrestrained, stop multitasking, and take your dog on a separate walk/jog. If you've had that run to unwind yourself, you can now just simply be there for/with your dog—to bear witness to and to truly connect with.

Your dog not only needs exercise, but they need to sniff as many things as possible during their limited time in the world (besides home). When being pulled to run, they are not able to do this, and it is sad, because sniffing is one of their truest joys. All sniffs tell a story that only the dog can read. Just because *you* do not have this sniffing superpower, realize that it exists and their ability to participate regularly in sniffing will only lend to their happiness. Plus, it makes you chill because it forces you to have patience—a win-win!

These are dog truths:

- All dogs need and deserve homes
- All dogs are perfect
- All dogs might not be a perfect fit for you or your family
- All dogs need love
- All (well, most) dogs need to have an active life
- All dogs are smart
- All dogs have compassion

Lisa Andrea Snyder

- All dogs have so much love in them that you may be shocked
- Dogs are funny
- Dogs are wise
- Dogs feel pain
- Dogs read the vibe in a room better than humans
- Dogs have empathy
- Dogs are characters
- Dogs are individuals
- Dogs are love

Before you decide to buy or adopt a dog, please know that they have real personalities and, most of all, needs. Please truly assess whether you can give the necessary care to a dog prior to acquiring one. Too many people that end up having a dog did so on an impulsive whim and got it so very wrong. Sadly, this results in dogs being marched back into a shelter or back to the breeder. People misunderstand and misinterpret dog behavior and then abandon their pets. This happens all too often, so it is worth reading all the chapters of this book (plus, it is a fun book!).

According to the Humane Society of the United States (as of September 2016), there were roughly seventy million stray cats and dogs living in the U.S., with only six to eight million of these animals finding their way into the nation's 3,500 shelters each year. My God, just think about those numbers. They are astounding.

There's a host of reasons for these numbers, but mainly it is because people *get it all wrong*, and a dog usually pays with their home, and sometimes their life.

In addition to misunderstood dog behavior leading to people surrendering their pets, here are some additional scenarios:

- A person opts for a relationship with a person who has allergies
- People move to places that do not allow pets

- People die and no one steps up to claim their beloved dog or cat. Sure, they are there to inherit or sift through a relative's belongings, but to hell with Scruffy, and sadly, the very last thing that an elderly relative would have wanted happens.
- People get dogs not realizing that having a dog can be costly, so if there is a diagnosis or event that is unaffordable, people do not step up. So, dogs end up in shelters, which are noisy and scary bad places for them, and sometimes these places kill them.

Decisions that are mostly made for convenience's sake are just some of the reasons that the shelters fill up. *We must all step up.* We simply must.

So, the question in the title asks, "Who is a dog person?" *You are!*

If you have always wanted a dog, think about it regularly (like ink-free fifty-year-olds think about tattoos), but have always stopped yourself because of, well, a host of reasons, you are a dog person! You just haven't had the dog yet.

Now that you are reading this, maybe this is you officially getting ready for your first dog. Maybe, just maybe, you had a dog as a kid but not since, so here you are for the first time in your adult life. Yay!

Read this book in its entirety, and get yourself a dog!

CHAPTER 3

There Really Are No Bad Dogs (But Some Are More Challenging Than Others)

THERE ARE SOME DOGS THAT come with certain challenges. You must think (just as if you were going to adopt a child with a handicap):

- Can I/we do this?
- Is this what I/we want?
- Am I/we about to embark on this more difficult journey out of guilt or obligation (perhaps you fostered with no intention of adopting)?

If you're part of a couple, is one of you more gung-ho about it? Perhaps you're just waiting for your partner to fall in line? This usually *does not* work. You must consider if there is a break-up, who will be the caretaker? Who will be the one to love your challenging dog? It really must be a joint venture, as it would be with children.

Now, back to my point—there really are no bad dogs. There are just millions of dogs in the world that don't have homes for a myriad of reasons: breeding and breeders, lack of spay/neuter programs, lack of understanding, and the dumping/abandoning at shelters (thinking they will get a home). Many dumped dogs (no matter how charming they are) do *not* have happy endings.

More scenarios:

- One family member develops an unnatural fear and so the dog goes off to the shelter.
- A dog nips a kid, and so off to the shelter (No! No! No!).
- People die and their relatives do *not* honor their wishes regarding their dearly beloved dog.
- Dogs are not spayed/neutered, resulting in healthy puppies and dogs getting euthanized. In this country alone, this dog massacre has reached crazy, unbelievable proportions.
- Breeders continue to breed, hence overbreeding, and people are persuaded to buy them. It is the age of the doodle, schnoodle, noodle dog.

Let's get over it. Yes, they too are wonderful, but each day a new hybrid is concocted and hyped. For this reason or that, shelter dogs have a *harder* time being seen. Also, most of these hybrids are not fully hypo-allergenic, as it takes three full generations for a dog to achieve that status. Cute? Yes! A-dog-able? Of course. But the sad truth is that they remove chances for shelter dogs to get homed.

Also, breeding can be cruel. Breeders may love the breed but are in fact just in it for the money. Sometimes when a dog is not up to "standard," *cruel* things happen (for the sake of the breed)—and, no, I shall not elaborate.

So, go mutt! Mixed breeds are less expensive, and they generally tend to be heartier and healthier. Why? By being a mix, they tend to get the best of the gene pools, and so there is a lower incidence of genetic disease.

Go to the shelter and decrease the madness by one! Lock eyes with the dog that melts your heart. Maybe you have the space in your heart and home for two? That should be an entire chapter (having multiple dogs), but you will probably arrive at this on your own one day. The more the merrier for some. One is plenty for others.

Learn about what your new rescue is, do a little research, and get into it. For example, I rescued a four-month-old Chihuahua mix from a Texas shelter a few years back. Once Luke arrived, he was precious (of course), and on our first day out walking, a stranger came up to me and said, "Oh, my God, a Basenji. I used to have one as a kid." The man was absolutely elated. This was a breed I had never even heard of nor would have sought out. Luke is the cutest, smartest, and most affectionate little guy (and, by the way, I have just described all dogs!).

If we as people just adopt and love—and adopt to love; if we can simply have and hold the dogs from this nation (and those imported from other nations) in our hearts and homes; if we stop looking for that perfect breed; if we stop clinging to our childhood pet; if we *stop* overbreeding and stop only seeking out Labs, retrievers, and doodles; if we are just mindful, even Zen about it; if we visit our local shelters, *lock eyes*, and commit to *one soul*, we can reduce/wipe out the stain of this nation that is the murder of millions of dogs.

Dogs in kill institutions, dogs rejected and thrown out like garbage—it is wrong, but *we can right it!* Fifty-five hundred animals are killed in U.S. shelters *every day* (millions per year)!

This is a quote from *One Green Planet*:

Adopting an animal into your family requires a great deal of dedication and commitment. When we bring an animal into our home, we are telling them that they are free to live without fear or abandonment for the rest of their lives. Sadly, many animals do not get the forever home and forever family they once trusted, and they end up scared, confused, and sad in shelters across the world. Although there are some legitimate reasons why animals are surrendered to shelters, like the death or illness of their caretaker, many animals are relinquished to shelters for the mere convenience of people.

There are no bad dogs!

CHAPTER 4

Adoption

THIS IS THE BIGGEST POINT: When you go to a shelter to find "your" dog, the dogs you see are not exactly at their best. How many people come away saying "too much barking," "too hyper," and "seemed stressed"?

Of *course*, wouldn't you be stressed?

I would take it one step further and propose the idea that dogs—smart, sweet, and super intuitive—*know* that when people come to observe them that this could be their ticket out of the noisy, barren madness. Just the sheer thought of that makes them crazy with joy. (Okay, I'm a bit out on a limb here, but surely you catch my drift, yes?)

They see you; they want to jump into your arms. They want to run after a thousand balls in an open field. They want to sleep on your bed (and if even part Chihuahua, dream of burrowing under the covers with you).

All these thoughts and dreams are coursing through their imaginations, fueling (possibly) their worst behavior. They are jumping, barking, and possibly drooling. They may in fact act aggressive. They are desperate and unfortunately acting it (and no one likes desperate).

Also note that the opposite can occur. When I adopted my now fifteen-year-old dog Beatrice (Bea) from the Newark Humane Society in 2007, I had seen her online, fell in love, and immediately drove there. She (then named Paisley) was not like the hyper droolers I mentioned before; no, she was lethargic. Why? She was depressed and had all but given up. She even had a goopy eye. She was rolled up in such a small little ball, and I could feel that she was so, so sad. I was not about to judge this (and I hardly knew anything all those years ago), but I recalled the look of joy that was somehow captured in her online photo. Her soul had spoken to me, and so I proceeded with abandon. I was a tad nervous about her health (and her eye, which later the tech assured me was normal for this type of environment).

The takeaway from all of this is that please, please, *please*, give these souls a chance—the chance they deserve.

How would you feel if you had to endure all that they did? How would you behave when people came to inspect you when you were at your possible worst?

Remember that the lethargy or hyperactivity is probably just a huge case of "Get me outta here"!

For truly these are God's creatures. They were more than likely born unwanted and have suffered tremendously. If they live to tell the tale, they will say it to you in gratitude. They will pay you in loyalty, salty kisses, and a specific kind of grace that only the dog beholds. They will look at you, and you will know that you did the right thing. I *promise* you!

When you have your day of visiting shelters, please proceed with care. Do not be rushed or in a hurry. Your intention is to find your family's newest member or your personal soulmate. Go deep inside yourself; focus and feel the energy. Feel *their* energy, and take your time! This is something that we all *always* need to work on, that need to stop rushing. And remember, every dog is an individual.

Adoption day is a *very* special day. Expect that you will lock eyes with a dog, a dog whose soul will change your life/lives forever for the better. *You will fall in love!*

CHAPTER 5

Food and the Proper Feeding of Your Dog(s)

THERE ARE DIFFERENT SCHOOLS OF thought on the subject of the feeding of dogs, so I am going to tell you what I have experienced. People have large differences of opinions on what I suggest, so I sincerely advise that you take my reading suggestion mentioned below.

Dogs are natural foodies.

Not just because they are dogs and we think that they will eat anything, but they truly feel elation by the mere mention of a treat. They stare at you lovingly (okay, drooling) while you prepare their plate. So, for a dog (the truest of foodies) to subsist solely on brown crunchy cereal (a.k.a. kibble) is a big mistake—health-wise *and* joy-wise.

I implore you to read up on what kibble really is and how it is not optimal nutrition, nor exciting, for them. There are so many wonderful, healthy ingredients that are inexpensive to buy that are super healthy for your dog to consume—ingredients that can *really* nourish your dog.

The dog food companies have gotten savvy. When sweet potatoes were initially trending in the dog food market, I thought "Why not just feed your dog actual sweet potato?" If you learn how to make food that is simple and economical, all you need is a little time. The sweet potato is just one example.

While dry dog food is more interesting than in years past (at least the marketing is more creative), and by this I mean it is somewhat more nutritious than it has been, nothing can be better or more nutritious than a fresh, homemade meal.

Most people feed their dogs breakfast and dinner, yes?

Feed your dog the dry food for breakfast, but add a little ground flax (a natural fiber and tasty too) and some low-sodium or sodium-free broth (any kind, even vegetable). This meal then becomes so much more fun for them. Why not a tad of shredded cheese to top it off? Or a dollop of cottage cheese? Voilà! You have just added to the enjoyment of your dog's life. They really do appreciate it. Truly!

On a side note, if you Google "How pet food is killing your dog" (from dailymail.co.uk) to gain knowledge about this topic, or simply search "Is commercial pet food bad for my dog?", many articles will pop up.

To quote just a few:

- "Canine nutrition expert says big business sells food unfit for dogs to eat"
- "Dogs should have a diet of raw meat, raw bones, and veggies"
- "Dog food industry began as way of making money from unwanted products"
- "Processed dog food could cause serious harm to the pets that eat it"
- "Canine nutrition experts accuse the big dog food manufacturers of knowingly shortening the lives of millions of dogs a year"

Okay, you get it. The pet food giants literally do not have your dog's back! *So you have to!*

Dinner time is where I am personally a little over the top, as I have not fed my dogs canned food or average junk dog food their entire lives. Bea, my oldest female mutt, who I got at the Newark Humane Society in 2007 when she was just six months old, has been fed the special mixture I am about to share with you for her entire life. Bea is at top form at 15-plus years (just a little slow in the morning, like I am).

The concoction I create from scratch is *so* easy, I mean *so super easy*, but alas, not as easy as pouring brown cereal in a bowl. *So, be and stay committed!*

Here are the ingredients:

- **Meat**: Turkey, chicken, beef. Raw, cooked lightly, or fully cooked.
- **Fish**: In the canned fish aisle in your grocery store, canned mackerel or canned salmon. I alternate. Salmon usually ranges between $2.99 and $9. I don't know what the difference is, but I assume it's all the same. This canned salmon can be opened and kept in a Tupperware container with all its juice filled with healthy and oily fatty acids. Mackerel is approximately $2.35 per can and comes in lots of juicy and oily broth. These small fish do have bones, but they are 100 percent edible for dogs. They disintegrate when touched, so do not worry. You can alternate or just do one, but most people like the lighter price of the mackerel.
- **Sweet Potato**: As soon as the pet companies caught on, they started including it in the commercial brands, so why not just bake them and serve fresh? Dogs love them!
- **Other Veggies**: Chopped frozen spinach or chopped frozen string beans (easy). Really, anything you want, including carrots and leafy greens; just make sure that you chop them small so your dog can digest them (or throw them in the food processor to create blended pulp). You can also use the pulp from juicing carrots and other veggies if you are a juicer. Experiment to see what your dog likes, loves, or hates.

Note that I always make it with just the three primary ingredients—meat, fish, and sweet potato. I'm trying to convey that this is easy and that you need only exert *minimal* effort.

I mix it all up together and then make single servings, like patties, which I can remove daily from the freezer and move to the fridge (on a plate or in a bowl for leakage), and they will be perfectly defrosted by dinner.

You can add ground flax seed, low-sodium broth, cottage cheese, shredded cheese, or just use the meat, fish, and sweet potato combo. Add warm water, mix, and serve.

I would also recommend olive oil daily (even just a tad), but if you are serving your dog the canned fish with the oils, that provides them with sufficient essential fatty acids.

Organ meat is very good for them as well. From all the reading I have done, it is not that easy to digest, as it is extremely high in protein, so it's good if you make this on occasion; it's a delightful treat for them. I primarily use chicken liver, sometimes beef, but I prefer the chicken liver because, after I cook it, I use the container it came in to store it in the fridge. I always sauté this until it is firm (it is kind of gross), and truthfully my dogs have loved it cooked and have even removed it from the food bowl when it was raw—to play with, *not* to eat.

The information available on serving your beloved dog a raw diet (and this goes for dogs of all shapes and sizes) is plentiful. I started more than thirty years ago with a book by a vet named Dr. Ian Billinghurst. This veterinarian and raw food specialist is known to many affectionately as Dr. B. It was 1993 when I read his book *Give Your Dog a Bone*. It was my introduction to the BARF (bones and raw food) diet when I got my first dog, Bogie.

This diet is designed for those who want easy-to-read, common-sense guidance on feeding for maximum health, low cost, and low environmental impact. It is inspired by the observation that dogs and cats fed a natural whole food diet are far healthier than when fed cooked and processed foods.

For those of you who have literally no time and are kind of laughing at all the above because "There's just no way, man," speak to your independently owned pet store that you frequent; speak to a person who *really* knows the raw deal—a person who can have an actual conversation about feeding raw, as most people have *no* idea. I really suggest reading Dr. B's book. Once I did all those years ago, I really understood, and obviously it stuck with me. People need to know and stop simply believing that all those ingredients in dog cereal and canned food are healthy.

Stop blindly trusting. If you are new to all things dog, *do not blindly trust.*

Making food may be time consuming, as it is for ourselves, but just like anything else, once it becomes a routine, you can do it in your sleep. Also, if you have a down day at home, like a Sunday, you can whip up a batch for the week, and then all you do is a daily defrost. Easy! I have seen dogs that have had skin conditions clear up in under two days on a better diet. It's the same for allergies too. Not always, but the chances are better for dogs to heal from their genetic and environmental woes when their diet is super clean and truly nourishing—again, just like us!

Three ingredients, that is all: meat, fish, and sweet potato (and the optional ground flax and green, if you want to add more).

Remember to occasionally add organ meat (I do it one week a month).

If you do not wish to mess around with/touch ground meats, visit your local pet store, as they now carry tubes of frozen meat. There are different brands that utilize different meats, and some are even already mixed with vegetables; some have both veggies and organ meat. These are usually a little more money, and it is cheaper to add this at home. Inquire about the quality of your choices, see what ingredients are listed and in what order, and make that purchase.

When you purchase the meat in a frozen tube, wait until it is a tad thawed, enough to get a large knife through it (I find a bread knife does the trick nicely), to cut it up into burger-size portions. Then freeze them individually. This has proven to be the easiest method (if you require utter ease), and I have done it all. Before you leave for work, throw an individual frozen "burger" into the fridge, and it will be perfectly thawed by dinner time.

In two containers in the fridge, you will have:

1. Fish from the can with all its oily juices
2. Roasted (baked) sweet potatoes

It just takes a couple of moments to throw the various ingredients into a bowl. Add a sprinkle of ground flax seed and then the warm water, so it seems like more and because some dogs do *not* drink enough water.

You may post on Instagram and spread the word.

#Dogsarefoodies
#BARFdiet
#Homemadedogfood

I am, of course, goofing around a little bit here, as I am a bit older and social media is *not* a natural for me, but I have done it. It's what we do now. We share because we care. Happy preparing!

Dry Food Tips

Buy a high-grade dog food, meaning that the first three ingredients are *not* fillers!

1. Carbohydrates should never be the first ingredient. Dogs are carnivores, so you want their diet to be made up of mostly meat proteins.
2. Avoid dry food with a high soy content, as soy is not good for a dog's endocrine system.
3. It's *all* about the first few ingredients, first and second being actual meat sources like beef, chicken, salmon, turkey, etc.

The meat that ends with the word "meal" can be a confusing subject. While we more than likely assume that meat meal is low-quality and therefore less healthy than real whole meat, this is not necessarily true. High quality meat meal can be an even higher source of protein, because in the making of meal, meat is cooked and all the excess water evaporates. What is then left is a higher concentrated protein.

Naturally, as with anything else, there are good and bad products. There is a range from extremely high quality that is a rich source of natural protein to meals that are comprised of waste products that can include funky animal parts like hooves and bones—the parts a dog would *not* eat even if they were to stumble upon a carcass in the wild.

It's always good to remember that pet companies originally started out by realizing they could sell the parts that were prior garbage. That was the premise to what is now a multi-billion-dollar-a-year industry. If you think that these companies would not cut corners (sometimes carelessly), and even sometimes maliciously, you would be wrong.

"Meals" To Avoid
- Meat and bone meal
- Chicken by-product meal
- Meat by-product meal
- Animal meal
- Animal by-product meal
- Meat meal

"Meals" That Are Good
- Beef meal
- Chicken meal
- Turkey meal
- Venison meal
- Lamb veal
- Duck meal

Especially stay away from any dog food that uses by-products. These are an especially unhealthy choice. Since I have always had different size dogs, I opt for the smaller dry food size. Dogs' teeth can get expensive, and if you have a senior dog, using the smaller size kibble is wise. Plus, it doesn't matter if you feed a larger dog the smaller size.

Some of you may encounter a dog that does not chew their food—they simply lap it up and swallow it. Personally, I cannot stand when dogs eat too fast, because there is a good chance that they will throw it all up, but it could also be a sign that chewing hurts, in which case the smaller size is better. Always have the vet check their teeth during their annual exam.

Note: There are bowls designed to slow down your dog's eating habit. Look for a slow feeder bowl at the pet store, or search online. Very crafty indeed!

So, for the morning dry meal, I add ground flax (I just reach into the bag and hand measure; it gets to be second nature). If you want to be precise, add somewhere between a teaspoon and a tablespoon, depending on the size of your dog. If your dog naturally has loose stool, add a pinch more. No amount is too much for this hearty-tasting fiber, but no more than a heaping tablespoon is necessary.

Other add-ons include:

Olive Oil (just a dollop)

From OliveOilTimes.com: "These monounsaturated fats will not only keep *your* heart healthy but could also keep your dog living longer. Potential benefits include the prevention of cardiovascular disease, diabetes, cancer, and excess weight gain, and . . . a healthier immune system."

According to Rover.com: "Studies have also found olive oil's link to brain health and joint health. Both are important for senior dogs, who can suffer from hip dysplasia, elbow dysplasia, arthritis, and osteoarthritis.

"Olive oil doesn't just keep dogs feeling good, it helps them look good too. The omega-3 fatty acids help moisturize the skin and prevent flakes from returning."

This according to PetGuide.com: "Recommended dose is 1 teaspoon of olive oil per 20 pounds of body weight per meal, mixed in with your dog's regular wet or dry food."

Eggs

Cooked or raw once or twice a week, it's a great protein and great for a shiny coat. It's also a great way to recycle a family's breakfast leftovers.

As per DogsNaturallyMagazine.com: "In addition to protein, feeding eggs to your dog is an easy way to offer them a range of nutritional support."

Eggs provide many key nutritional components including vitamin A, riboflavin, folate, vitamin B12, iron, selenium, and fatty acids.

For those of you who might worry about the Salmonella risk, your dog is well-equipped to handle the bacteria in raw foods. I have fed a raw egg a week to my dogs over the years, and they lap it up and have very shiny coats.

I feed them eggs that I eat, which are organic and from free-range chickens. I do this because I have always tried to be healthy, and eggs are relatively inexpensive. Once I learned that a lot of the companies (if not all of them) spray their eggs with a chemical to make them appear shiny, I *stopped* buying regular eggs.

Broth

Bone broth, beef broth, chicken broth, and vegetable broth. Use them for additional flavoring and as a great addition to cajole hesitant eaters. Just be aware that broth has a high sodium content. Use a low-sodium broth, and don't overdo it.

Coconut Oil

One of the world's few saturated-fat vegetable oils that seems to be good for everything, the recommended dose for dogs is one teaspoon per thirty pounds of dog.

There is literally a sea of information espousing the positive benefits of this oil.

As per WholeDogJournal.com: "Watch for changes in your dog's energy, skin, coat, breath, and body odor. In dogs, the medium-chain fatty acids in coconut oil balance the thyroid, helping overweight dogs lose weight and helping the sedentary feel energetic. As a bonus, coconut oil improves any dog's skin and coat, improves digestion, and reduces allergic reactions."

To learn more about this amazing oil, please read the article "How Coconut Oil Benefits Your Dog's Health" in the online magazine *Whole Dog Journal*. It is truly informative!

Please always remember, as it is the same with us humans that *consistency is key!*

Cottage Cheese or Shredded Cheese

These cheeses are perfect to top off and finish your dog's dish! Cheese is high in calcium and protein. If you notice, almost every commercial treat claims to be flavored with cheese, so why not just use actual cheese? I buy shredded in bulk; it is cheaper, and I can use it as well.

There are many other additional ingredients that could be placed inside of their bowl. Just use your imagination, from ground flax to cooked carrots. Some dogs even love apples.

When you are scraping plates from dinner into the garbage, have a Tupperware container handy so that you don't needlessly throw away a piece of chicken or some other doggy edible. Rinse off sauces and other *schmutz* so it becomes dog appropriate. These odds-and-ends foods do not need to be fed to your dog immediately. Sometimes there are a lot of "extras," so rinse and place these in a special container or else your dog might gain unnecessary weight.

Life would be so much less fun and interesting without meals to enjoy. I have always thought that dogs were overlooked in this department. We all know that dogs can sometimes be disgusting (okay, gross), as they are attracted to things we cannot fathom, from the eating of spring dirt for what they could be lacking nutritionally to cat shit right out of the litter box. While we cannot comprehend it, dogs are keen, sense-driven wolves to their core. What we term disgusting is a superior dining experience to them.

To conclude, and to make one of my biggest points of this book, it is what is fed to a dog that *truly* matters. Dogs know when something is status quo (may stay in the bowl for hours) and when a meal is beyond amazing (eaten with gusto and on the spot).

A breakfast meal of a good dry with the added ingredients listed in this chapter and a dinner that has them jumping for joy . . . well, this lifestyle is life-extending! Aren't we for anything that can extend the life of our dog? Again, it's the same for humans—excellent high-quality food and as much happiness as possible equals *longer life!*

You may be reading this and thinking to yourself that with all that's going on in the world that the feeding of an exciting and healthy meal could be deemed a luxury issue and *not* a true concern. I get that, but this book is titled what it is for a reason, and for this reason . . .

Meals should be a masterpiece!

My three dogs sit and wait while I prepare their food. They know what's about to occur, and they are grateful and full of love. I feed them as best I can because I love them so. I want them to enjoy every moment of their too-short lives. Humans can extend their lives with good nutrition, and dogs' lives can be extended as well. I am not a doctor, but I am alive and in tune with my own body. I know that GIGO (garbage in, garbage out) is real.

CHAPTER 6

Exercise Equals Joyous Creatures

IF YOU BUY, ADOPT, OR somehow acquire a dog, you *must* adjust your life (lives) to include a daily exercise regimen. Dogs, like humans, get pent up, and like us, they can be destructive (and/or become miserable and depressed) when no endorphins are released. To note, I am not condoning running or cycling with your dog with them being pulled or pressured to keep up. Dogs need to stop, sniff (sometimes *a lot*), and do their business, but they can't if you are pulling them.

To all the super-high-energy motivated athletes out there, do *your* thing and be in it fully. When you are done doing you, spend dedicated time with your patient and loving best friend and give them *their* daily dose of exercise. Or take your dog out for their time *before* you run yourself. Think of it as even more exercise, both physically and mentally. It is a true discipline to put another's needs before your own, and this time gives you a chance to chill and switch gears—*to literally walk before you run.*

Dogs are also quite fond of (good) excitement, so make your dog even happier when you are in the "going out" mode. Accomplish this with high-pitched songs and declarations to your pup. Sing to them in your love voice, tell them you love them, and say, "Let's go out! Let's go out!" They will be doggie shrieking with joy. Luke, my Chihuahua/Basenji, is literally so happy that he cries when I make a big deal out of going out, let alone as we approach his happy place, be it the trail, the dog run, or sometimes just as he enters the vehicle that transports him.

Dogs feed off of our emotions, so be happy.

Lisa Andrea Snyder

I know that mornings are difficult, especially if you are a family with kids, and more than likely your dog gets a quick goal-oriented walk. Maybe not even one full lap around the block? Then right back in? Then they sit around all day (even if there is a yard), *all day* without their people. They are lonely and sometimes can be destructive. Some dogs sleep all day long, and you suppose that they just like to sleep? Wrong! You could not be more wrong. Dogs (again, like us) need to be engaged, need to look forward to things, and they really need adventure.

When you picture your dog from now on, picture them in a Girl or Boy Scout uniform or as a firefighter or as Super Dog! Don't picture them snoozing happily all day long because they just love to sleep. For God's sake, they just slept the whole night!

Know that canines are athletes, even the tiny ones. They need exercise just as much as their larger counterparts. The littles are sometimes rigged with a super-high-strung nervous system. These are the dogs that are prone to getting the least amount of exercise, with some of their owners putting down wee-wee pads for them to use inside. There are little dogs that are sought after due to the misinformation that they don't need any exercise because they are small.

Nothing is further from the truth!

These little dogs were a welcome addition to my Canine Adventure business. Sometimes, I had to cajole the owners to let me take them along with their bigger dog. I would venture to say that 90 percent of the time these littles are highly adventurous big dogs trapped in small bodies, not so fragile, and can play with big dogs.

Contrary to most people's fears, dogs have an innate sense of things. They are spatially brilliant. I mean, who else can run fifty miles an hour tangled up in racy play with another couple of dog pals and *not* smash into that tree? Littles have that exact same ability/capability! They just know. And if you have a dog with small children, they just know (mostly!). They just know how to mouth play without biting, because dogs are instinctual. They are smart, wise, and affectionate, and we should *trust* them more! The more we trust them, the more their collective experiences accumulate and add to their brilliance, which contributes even more to their instincts.

What I am trying to say is that the more we allow our dogs to participate fully in *our* lives, the better, happier, and more relaxed they tend to be.

Exercise your dog (exercise yourself)!

CHAPTER 7

Poop (Yep, a Chapter on Poop)

JUST LIKE HUMANS, DOGS NEED to poop, and *no* dog should have to wait too long to go. Imagine if we couldn't go just at the precise moment we needed to! You gotta go when you gotta go, right?

Our dogs are so darn considerate (except for the dog, *that* dog, who nudges your sound-asleep body at 5 a.m.). Aside from *that* dog, they are usually on our schedule for everything.

A good and fair routine ensures that you don't leave your dog with a full bowel. This is simply *not* nice or fair. Even if you think they can go nine hours, and even if they can *and* even if they do, they are not holding it in because it's easy. They are being considerate team players. Sadly, some dogs may even be used to certain repercussions or punishment (in a less forgiving and less compassionate home), such as yelling or, God forbid, anything else.

There can be side effects in dogs that are forced to hold in urine and feces. In today's world of Google . . . well, I won't go there, but please do look it up. In essence, forcing dogs to hold their bladders for too long increases the risk of urinary tract infections. The books refer to dogs needing to pee three to five times per day—again, kind of like us.

Go Out Before Breakfast

There are some people that feed their dogs before they take them out in the morning. To this I respond (besides OMG!) imagine if you had to eat before you even peed, let alone pooped. People do this because they don't really think about it.

33

It's a convenient habit, and because they think that if they feed their dog and then take them out after, they are hopeful that this poop will include breakfast.

It's simply not true!

Breakfast has not even begun to digest yet, so in fact what their dog experiences is a tad of confusion. "I am a dog and I love to eat, and I am being fed, so I will eat." The truth is that they *really* need to get out shortly upon awakening to pee *and* poop. Please, realize this. Your dog will be digesting breakfast after you leave for work, and breakfast will be released in their afternoon walk.

Dinner

It is the same with dinner. If your schedule has you coming home later than you'd like, please do not feed your dog immediately upon arriving home, taking them out after. They are in the need of exercise, peeing, and pooping (if no dogwalker or friend came by midday), so get out there! *They have to go!* They are home all day, probably strolling to their water bowl occasionally, and they need to go.

Poop Consistency

Your dog shouldn't have to strain, and your dog should not have loose stool. Poop should be easy to eliminate, soft but firm and with no blood. Occasionally (and this is normal), poop can seem to be encased in mucous. This is okay, but if it happens *all* the time, get to your vet and bring a stool sample. Mucous can be a common symptom of inflammatory bowel disease (IBD), signs of parasites, autoimmune disorders, and even cancer. It can also be nothing; it just happens to most dogs from time to time. If you see it frequently, don't be alarmed, just see your vet.

Dogs Eat Weird Stuff

Grass, dirt, mud, cat poop, bird poop, bird food, all sorts of random things, so of course their poop consistency is affected.

If you don't think your dog is slick enough to sneak in some of these tasty delicacies on their time out with you, you would be wrong. That is why (as per another chapter in this book) it is super beneficial to be fully present. They are quick, and they can even hide a "treat" in their mouth to save for later.

If you see your dog doing the slide (occasionally it is normal) as a regular occurrence, your dog probably has worms or some sort of parasite. He/she may also just need some anal friction, possibly to release a piece of grass or something irritating their anal glands. Annual vet exams include anal gland release.

Okay, here's a story. When I had my first dog, shortly after acquiring him, I saw an actual string hanging part way out of his tush. I had to (I know . . . ew!) pull it out, and there it was—a tampon. Oh, my God, my new beautiful dog who I thought had a ton of class ate a used and discarded tampon from a city street or from a local park that we frequented. This happened way before I was the experienced dog person that I am now, and I shall *never* forget it. Ugh! To note, Bogie was not embarrassed at all! I felt weird telling people at the time, but I later learned that it was not so abnormal. Just try to keep an eye on what your dogs ingest.

If you have a child or children, *always* stress the importance of what to feed and what *not* to feed the family dog, and sometimes you *must* stress to the kids or spouse or dogwalker to *not* give treats. Overweight dogs are not a sign of a loved or pampered dog, as dogs must endure all the health problems humans do when they are overweight. Food *is* love, but show that love in the meals that you feed them. Treat-driven dogs are a cliché, and your dog is *so* much better than that.

The reason people end up believing that dry food (kibble) is so good for their dog is because there is a consistency to their poop. In very busy lives, no one has time for anything other than a quick, easy, and usually voluminous poop! We may even unconsciously equate their colon health with this large pile of seemingly healthy looking sh*t. Truth is, the more that comes out, the probability is that a good amount of their food was not properly processed, digested, and absorbed.

Lisa Andrea Snyder

Remember GIGO (garbage in, garbage out). The raw food diet is more easily absorbed into their system, as it is healthy and completely nourishing—hence less to exit stage left. The poop may not be the size and shape that you are used to seeing from dry brown cereal food, but trust that your dog will be healthier and experience less urgency.

I know that when I (a very healthy eater) take in food that is not my norm, my body is quick to get rid of it. Garbage in, garbage out!

CHAPTER 8

Weather

IN SOME WAYS, IT IS easier having human children, because you do not have to walk them in the rain, hurricanes, snowstorms, or blizzards. Dogs will go out in these conditions when prompted, but sometimes they *do* need to be coerced.

The question is, will you?

From the start, let them know that no matter the weather conditions, you have them covered, that you will be providing them with relief even when they fear the thunder. Get them in the habit of going *fast*!

For those of you who say "My dog will just not go out in the rain" or some such thing, well then, make sure that you have a wee-wee pad, but note that most dogs will *not* use them when they are only used occasionally. If they are not regularly used, dogs simply do not catch on.

So, get out there no matter what, before these types of narratives become an excuse. Make it a fun and quick adventure (out of respect for their bladders and colons). Big whoop! We take a walk with our rain gear and umbrella. Your dog can also have rain gear! That's life, rain and crap weather being a part of it.

Some of the best memories over the years with dogs have been completely unexpected, and yes, weather related. Dogs love romping in the snow; it's huge fun for them, especially seeing your dog experience it for the first time. Amazing! Then, getting caught in a deluge of rain can also be fun, wildly so.

Lisa Andrea Snyder

Running in the Rain with Your Dog!

How often in our carefully crafted lives do we have that experience of getting caught in the rain? Practically never. *Enjoy* what is a rare and natural experience. We don't melt!

That said, pouring down rain with high winds and sleet is not so much fun, and it's easy to not want to go out. Dogs will figure out hopefully to go fast. Try to create a bad weather walk pattern so it becomes familiar—much shorter than usual, but at least they are getting the opportunity to relieve themselves.

Out of all the years while having dogs in the Northeast, there have only been a handful of times that it poured day and night nonstop. Now we have weather apps, and it's as simple as glancing at your phone (which is mostly correct) and adjusting your walk time according to a break in a bad weather system.

No one wants to go out when the weather is horrific, including your dog. Just know that they *do* have to go, and you will have to craft a routine.

Know all the stuff—the good, the bad, and the weatherly!

Little Side Note

I always completely towel off my dogs (that's twelve paws) each time we return from such a walk. Unscented baby wipes work *great* on the paws, and I use a towel for their paws, limbs, and undercarriages. It's an act that bonds you. My dogs play fight for who gets the towel treatment first. It's adogable! Try it!

Also, Google "paw plunger." You will thank me.

CHAPTER 9

Love and Engagement

THIS MIGHT JUST BE THE chapter you skim or gloss over but trust me when I tell you that it may be one of the most important. I guess I could have called this chapter "Mindfulness (With Your Dog)," but I am so sick of that word these days. It's everywhere.

Once again, despite the fast-paced nature of our lives—the carpooling, the running to our yoga class so we can remain calm through it all—we just need to stay mindful of our dogs. They can never *ever* be the creature on the floor at home waiting ever so patiently (even if on a comfy bed) for their turn in our day. What we perceive as patience in *not*!

Think of this quote from Henry David Thoreau (1817–62): "The mass of men leads quiet lives of desperation. What is called resignation is confirmed desperation." So, I have repurposed it for this little book: "Most dogs lead lives of quiet desperation."

And there you have it.

Quiet Desperation

Whether polite and mellow, barking and frantic, or outright destructive, dogs need, dogs deserve, *and* dogs must have their turn—their turn to be active, to have a plan—a play and exercise plan.

When you are parents of small children, part of your caring for them is to tire them out so you can chill, right? Parents know just how much energy some kids have, and it is in their best interest to engage them to deplete that energy. It is off to a play

40

group, the park, or that myriad of activities that you spend too much time chauffeuring them around back and forth.

It is like us with exercise. We are our best selves when well exercised. It's good for our bodies and our minds. So, it is with that very same intel that I am reporting to you that you *must* do the same for your dog(s).

Lisa Andrea Snyder

It is crucial!

The shelters are *full*, and much of that has to do with the undeniable fact that people that do not know much about dogs get dogs, do *not* give dogs what they need, and then *discard* dogs when they behave badly and/or act destructively.

There is a simple solution (I told you this was a short chapter):

Love Your Dog and Engage Your Dog =
Happy Life = No Destructive Behavior =

Never Get Rid Of Your Dog =
Decrease In Shelter Population

CHAPTER 10

Massage and the Importance of Touch

WE ALL NEED LOVE, AND we all need touch.

Dogs are no different. Even though we love them and care for them as best we can, sometimes we forget to bond through focused, conscious touch. Try to find the time to massage your young or old dog limb by limb, slowly and carefully, and focus as you do. If you are slow and mindful, you can see if they have any areas that cause them pain. This is useful information to have. Focused touch and massage are such a wonderful way to bond with your pup or senior dog and really does a lot in the way of calming.

Dogs can't meditate (I don't think), but they reach bliss through being held, touched, and massaged, the effects being undeniable. In the beginning, especially if you adopt/rescue a dog from a shelter, they may be leery and act untrusting. You can see this on their trepidatious faces, and you can feel it in their body language, as they may get a bit stiff or rigid (probably an act of protecting themselves—possibly they were abused?). Proceed slowly while you build trust. It is a great time to use your voice to speak to them lovingly and help to comfort them, to help them feel calm. The massage I am referring to is the straightening of a back or front leg so you can get into the upper portion of it, softly massaging strong and sometimes pent-up muscles. I sometimes get into their actual paws or gently rub their ribs, even getting in between them.

Dogs *love* this, but at first they may not. Initially, it can be weird for them. As you watch them receive your healing touch, you get to bear witness to them overcoming any fears while learning to trust and receive love. This goes a very long way. Doggie massage can improve blood flow, alleviate stress, and reduce pain if they have any. It can relax tight and sore muscles and may help to reduce the pain of sprains and strains (issues you may not even know they have).

I know that with all the hiking and running my girl Bea has done over her fifteen-plus years, her occasional limp can be easily remedied with on-the-spot massage. I simply locate what I think is the source and just start some gradual yet deep massage. I look at her and speak to her calmly to let her know I am going to fix her pain, and she has always seemed to be down with it. Your calming voice saying loving things helps as well.

Most times, Bea's limp goes from an acute and sad limp to nonexistent, with her being pain-free again. Mind you, I am *not* suggesting not going to your vet if a limp lasts days; just try to use the powers of your own intuition and massage first (and do not be afraid to get right in there).

Think of athletes in a professional sport with a massage therapist on hand to work out the kinks. That is what I am talking about here. It will be more instinctual for some people, but it is a skill you can acquire. Just be present and focus.

The only time Bea did not succumb successfully to my massage was when she had a thorn in her paw. Luckily, I saw it and plucked it out. I highly recommend doing regular body scans for lumps, bumps, ticks, and scabs. It is utterly amazing that these vibrant creatures do not get hurt more often. They do not run into trees, and their keen senses protect them from so much potential hurt. I have always watched them in amazement. Dogs—wonderful, joyous, love-filled, amazing dogs.

I am not a masseuse, and you don't have to be either. Some dogs might not get into the deeper tissue kind of touch and just prefer to be scratched and pet (like a human who prefers Swedish massage over Korean or Thai deep tissue massage). Preference for type of touch is personal. Fortunately, this lighter touch too, if done with proper focus, can be very bonding and is highly beneficial.

I am not referring to just a couple of pats or singular strokes while you say "good boy" or "good girl," but creating a time with just the two of you that you both look forward to. Yes, it's one more thing on your already overbooked agenda, and it's hard to schedule this time if you are lacking quality time with your kid(s), but your child ultimately goes to sleep (right?). Your dog can have you for five minutes, even just three. Plus, if you have high blood pressure, this can help to lower it.

All beings, canine and humans alike, crave touch! There is even a YouTube video where a woman had a pet bee, and she would pet this bee, and the bee was clearly enjoying it. Very weird, but very cool.

Imagine how our lives would change if even for just five or ten minutes each day or night, we knew we were going to be thoroughly loved and touched. It is healing and too easy *not* to do it.

So, touch and massage your dog!

CHAPTER 11

Riding in Cars with Dogs

DOGS LOVE GOING FOR A drive—for any length of time. If you have a reason to be in the car, from running out for milk to a full-blown day at a friend's, bring your dog with you and your family whenever possible.

Take any chance to make your dog feel included and happy!

I do realize that there are dogs that have bark issues and dogs that have car issues (as in getting them into the car or motion sickness). For those dogs, these are separate issues, and I do not suggest bringing them to places where they can ruin your time.

If you are a parent, you can bring your dog to a kid event, even if they stay in the car—though *not* in hot weather. Usually, dogs are not allowed at the multitude of sports fields you visit (soccer, baseball, football, etc.), but they are just so happy and satisfied to be a part of the gang. They are completely thrilled to be on the go *anywhere* with their family. They know that they are with you, and if you do this regularly and if you have a barker, this just may cure him or her of it. Often, dogs are just left at home while everyone else goes out into the day to do their stuff, to live their lives.

With COVID-19, this chapter may not be as relevant, but it is still good intel!

A Playful and Adventure-Seeking Go Dog

Even if you are just going to the store, the moment you say "Come on" or "Let's go," well, that is what your dog lives for.

Even if it is just to go smoke the cigarette that you swear you are not smoking around the corner.

That all stated, when you are planning your weekend, with kids or just by yourself, do something that your dog can be a part of, if possible. They do not want to be dumped at a kennel. A lovely car trip in autumn, winter, or spring, while you are hiking or shopping, they can more than likely be a part of it. So many more places are pet friendly now. Also, in these seasons, they can happily wait for you in the car. *It's the same thing as waiting at home!*

For all of you that live in hot states, I am not talking to you here. Never *ever* leave a doggie in a car in hot weather.

Bring your dog when you can!

CHAPTER 12

Dogs and Kids

DOGS AND KIDS TOGETHER ARE simply the best.

My favorite life memory is so simple: Being on my bed with my glorious nieces and my three dogs lying on top of us. Limbs and paws all together, intertwined. The giggling, the love, and the silly humor. Sometimes, merely the way your dog looks at you at these times can evoke gratitude, silliness, and incredulity at their depth.

Having members of both species in your home can be a lovely experience, but it can also be very taxing, so if you are a one-parent family, please do not feel pressured into acquiring a dog for your child. People do what I like to call "child pleasing," and it always rises to bite them in their arses. If you are the sole human responsible for a kid or kids, that is a great deal of work daily, so even if you have help, adding a dog and all that comes with that decision is not to be undervalued or overlooked. Dogs take time and energy, and simply put, you might *not* have extra to spare.

The good part of having both a kid, or kids, and a dog, if it is feasible, is the bond that they will have with their dog sibling. Parents need to train the kids *how* to have a dog, and this training should take place *before* the new family member is in the home. Everything from how to treat your new dog or pup to how the kids introduce their new pet to their friends, as sometimes dogs are possessive and treat *any* "outsider" as a threat.

There are basic things to consider—issues that new pet owners may never have even thought of. Please know and believe that this type of awareness helps dogs *stay* in their new homes. *This is the entire point of this book.*

You need to know what could possibly ruff-ruff-ruffle your dog's feathers, so to speak, because one unintentional wrong move and a kid could get really scared.

Dogs get overtired and sometimes need to take a break from play.

It does *not* take much for a child to spontaneously develop a fear of an animal; this happens a lot and is a big reason that dogs are given back to where they came from, and God forbid it was a kill shelter. Also, teach the kids not to overdo it with treats, because that really does matter. If you are trying to establish a routine for pooping and your dog is eating a whole bunch of treats that you are not aware of . . . you see where I'm going with this? Get the kids disciplined with doing their part (as they promised they would as part of the original condition for getting the dog), so that you, the parents, do not get angry, hangry, and resentful when it *all* falls on your shoulders, and as was mentioned earlier, *it will.*

If there are kids with any sort of emotional or psychological issues, teaching them to be extra gentle and appropriate with your new dog is critical. Even with few or no issues, kids can have the tendency to play rough and experiment on dogs and pups. I have heard stories from vets that include:

- Putting little toys into dogs' ears
- Cutting off their hair/fur with scissors
- Giving them medicine
- Tail pulling
- Making their collar super tight

This list goes on and on. Who would think that there would be such scenarios to consider, but just like childproofing a home in preparation for your child's toddler years, so must you safely (child)proof your home for your pets. Children are curious, active creatures, and they like to try things. Sometimes those things can hurt a dog.

If you suspect that your child is purposefully cruel to a dog (or cat or hamster) beyond what is considered innocent (as listed above), please *do not* ignore this. It more than likely will not stop and only progress. Take care of this immediately! *There is no excuse to ignore this type of behavior.*

Teach *all* kids that when play gets too rough it can result in the new dog/pup becoming wound up and possibly aggressive. Then the adults, possibly seeing only part of the story, decide that the dog must go. Perhaps a new dog owner wasn't completely sure about getting a dog to begin with. Maybe they are just looking for an excuse to return the dog. Therefore, as I mentioned in Chapter 3 (There Are No Bad Dogs), *all* parties in a household must be fully down with getting a dog. This dynamic accounts for literally millions of dogs being tossed out of families, and this dynamic is preventable. You, the owner *and* caretaker, need to be incredibly stern when it comes to how your child or children behave around the dog.

If you took on a rescue, they may be super sensitive to sound or overprotective in general (a common trait). There are literally so many ways your rescue dog or pup could be reeling from prior abuse or neglect. Sometimes you will not have one inkling of this. It could be a long-dormant trait or characteristic that can spontaneously and surprisingly erupt. Usually, these are not ideal surprises, but please expect them. They may not occur, but be ready for them. Protect your new dog or pup from being rendered homeless (again). This is all normal, and educating yourself is key. Teaching your children what is both acceptable and not acceptable is also key!

Some of you will think I am hyper vigilant regarding children, but you absolutely must make it your business to understand your dog and their *potential* behavior. It is only with this awareness that you become part of the solution while ceasing being potentially part of the problem. When strange or bad reactions are unexpected from your dog or pup, you *know* it is normal.

Your true understanding of dog behavior can prevent dogs and pups from being surrendered either back to where they came from or to the local shelter. These shelters may or may not be kill shelters, but it really doesn't matter, because no matter how wonderful you heard the place is, the situation itself can kill their spirit, and then they become even more at risk for having sad or bad behavior, *therefore lowering their adoptability!* Please be aware it is all connected!

Regarding how dogs are the ultimate protector: have you heard the term "nanny dog"? This was an original term for pit bulls (also referred to as bully dogs). In England, the Staffordshire bull terrier is nicknamed the "nanny dog" because of their reputation as a child's playmate and guardian. A nickname, yes, but an overall lovely situation that parents have in the backs of their minds when they think of getting a dog, and we *all* want this type of experience within our homes.

We all want the protector that a dog can be. I am of course not referring to leaving a child at home alone with the family dog (obviously), just that you will feel a form of protection naturally emanating from your dog. The sweetest, most docile dog can have strong instincts in protecting your family in a variety of potential situations.

That stated, you (and your family) must supply your dog with maximum respect in all the various ways I am discussing in this book, so that they can hone their innate instincts to the fullest and protect you and your family. In other words, a dog that gets no exercise, hardly enough attention, and must hold their bladder all day long—a great guard dog this does *not* make.

Dogs, very much like children must be taught. It is an investment of time and energy (just like kids), and you the parent(s) must be extraordinarily present. You must watch what goes on in your home with all animals that are new, because so much can go wrong. *Do not wait for a crisis to be reactive. Be 100 percent present!*

Be your new animal's spokesperson. Do *not* just turn your new pet over to the kids because kids are not responsible and have a natural curiosity that could even lead one to believe they are cruel (potentially). Keep it all in check. You are the responsible adult(s). You are responsible for the care and maintenance of your new animal. *You are responsible for their life, not the kids!*

Too many parents (again) "child please." It's a very modern way of raising kids, just giving them everything that they ask for that you can afford. If their friends have it, have one or have two, it is your duty to help your kids be one of the gang, right? No! It is your job to be there to explain that not every kid has a dog or an iPhone or the latest expensive game. Or a scooter, a bicycle, or expensive sneakers. The list goes on—it never stops—and you will be a hamster on that wheel, and even go into debt to keep your kids keeping up with the Joneses.

Never do it. Never. Especially when it comes to live fish, bunnies, hamsters, gerbils, birds, lizards, cats, dogs, horses, and goats! They are all sentient creatures that deserve to be safe. There are so many lessons you can take advantage of on the journey of acquiring a live animal. Be 100 percent present.

Also, dogs last a good long while—years, sometimes a decade and a half, perhaps two decades, usually just a few years short of your kids being in the house before college or another adventure. It is a gigantic decision! *It is not an experiment, because it cannot fail!*

You cannot be part of a dynamic that lands a dog in a terminal or dire situation. If you decide to do this, you must be committed. You must be the adult, and you must be 100 percent responsible!

To conclude, when the adult(s) lay down the rules and fully and competently oversee them, all the sentient creatures can live under one roof without fear. Each person, young and old, will be in full understanding that a dog is a living, breathing, loving soul that needs to be looked out for, because like each of us, they have their limits.

Once you commit, they are here to stay!

TOP: Pac Member Delaney—*Sentient creatures thrive in nature*

BOTTOM: Pac Member Daisy—*Seriously wondering when her next adventure is*

TOP: Pac Member Cyrus—*Proof a dog can be alpha and a pussycat*

BOTTOM: Pac Member Kika—*There is so much to do on daily adventures*

TOP: Pac Member Rosco—*There is always at least one extremely contemplative canine*

BOTTOM: Pac members lining up on a hike

TOP: Pac Member Molly the Hound—*Sometimes bolted, always came back*

BOTTOM: Pac Members Archie, Echo & Colby—*Small dogs especially need to run daily*

Pac Leader (me)—*Surrounded by love at dog run (no treats given during Pac play)*

Cattle Dogs are amazing—*Pac member Remy*

TOP: Friends chatting while traveling
BOTTOM: Dogs love to travel.

PLEASE CHECK OUT

WWW.THE CANINE AMERICAN.COM

Help put a dent in ending the dog meat trade.

CHAPTER 13

Dogs and Cats

LONG BEFORE I EVER HAD a dog, I considered myself a cat person, but I love all animals and was born to have them. Of course, it was inevitable and natural that I would have both, and currently I have three dogs and one cat—Bea, Pearl, Luke, and Max. Max was such a frisky paw-swiping kitten that I gave him the alternate name, Cat Bastard—or Cat B or CB for short. He is an indoor/outdoor tuxedo, and he prides himself on his fierce independence. That said, he almost always appears just in time to join the dogs' morning walk, and their late night walk too. I love and appreciate every second of this very specific magic.

I have never felt more in my element than when walking down a street, field, or trail with three dogs and a super confident black and white cat. He is adventurous and even runs at full speed at times. He likes to lag, and then he runs as fast as he can to catch up. That was mainly when we lived in Asheville, North Carolina, and had twenty acres to romp through. Max would also climb trees, and to watch a cat get down is also a treat to behold. It made me realize that we do not usually see cats like this. It is beautiful.

Many people do not agree with a cat that lives indoors and outdoors (and yes, I've lived in apartments and have had indoor only cats, but this book is about dogs). To sum it up, cats need to live their best lives too. Not all cats can, but some will only be happy if let out! It's a personal lifestyle choice and a decision that should be made with each individual cat. Plus, I felt like Cat Bastard would kill me if I didn't let him outside. Moving on . . .

Lisa Andrea Snyder

While dogs and cats mainly ignore each other, they are somewhat just fooling us humans, because they secretly love and long for each other's company and attention. I have witnessed them running after one another playfully, sleeping together, and every day, two out of three of my dogs playfully nibble on Cat Bastard. I, their human, am always in awe! During this light nibbling, my cat is on his back in full on enjoyment. He especially loves the attention physically. I also think that dogs know that if push came to shove, any cat could rip their eyeballs out, as the animal kingdom is keen and intuitive. Animals know just how far they can go. It's silly fun and humorous to witness.

Cats and dogs are opposite creatures. Cats are slick and wise, sleeping a lot during the day (always with one eye open). Dogs are more needy of their human caretakers. Cats seemingly couldn't care less, but when they are affectionate or in need of your attention, take note, as they really do need you after all! When your cat is emotionally and/or physically needy, deal that love out and deal it out freely. Dogs and cats and kids in the yard. What could be better?

This all stated, I must be a responsible writer about dogs and cats and emphasize that not all dogs can or should be trusted with cats. Ask any veterinarian about some of the cats that come into their offices with injuries from dog attacks and vice versa.

When adding a dog or cat to your family (established pack), acknowledge that while it will probably be fine for the cat or dog, take the time to properly expose them to one another. They experience fear, jealousy, territorialism, and anxiety just like human children. You wouldn't get a dog and just leave him or her alone in a room with your child, and this is the *same* thing. Supervise, observe, and make decisions on how to proceed wisely and mindfully.

Cats and dogs do seem to have a natural affinity for one another. It just takes a period of adjustment time. Also, to note, just because your cat is all hissy and acting "freaked," it does not mean that is the be all and end all. *This is how they communicate. This is how they sound.*

62

Cats and dogs together are a natural most of the time.

Lisa Andrea Snyder

Just acknowledge that adding a new dog or cat to the family will take some getting used to. It takes time for them to adjust to this life change, this addition, because it really is a big deal for each of them. You, being the grown up and ultimately the one responsible for everyone being safe and happy, must be extremely aware of this somewhat jarring and life-changing event. It's a very big deal when a family brings home a new baby, and it is also a very big deal when you add a new pet. When dynamics change, be conscious . . . eyes open!

Dogs and cats have very different boundaries in general and with each other. When you have one and then acquire the other, you *never* just leave them alone with one another or leave them unattended.

Have I overstated the point here?

Don't worry so much when your cat or the new feline acts completely whacko! It's crazy just how weird a cat can behave. We all know that compared to dogs, cats are the stranger species; just watch how kittens play.

Dogs are usually *very* excited to meet a cat, *but* the exception is the dog who clearly has the instinct to kill a cat. This should be known prior to the new addition, but if not, it should be obvious and clearly not the type of dog to bring into your home if there is a cat. Just try not to confuse this severe behavior with that of an excited puppy meeting your mature family cat. This cat will hiss like you will have never witnessed before. *This is normal.*

As far as having both a cat and a dog, it sure is entertaining! Some of my heartiest belly laughs have come from watching these two interact. Highly recommended!

CHAPTER 14

Boarding

NO! NO! NO! NO! DON'T do it! (If you can avoid it.)

Unless you are 100 percent sure that you have found an amazing place that is exceptionally caring and committed to your dog, and that the business does what they advertise, it is best not to board your dog. Online, you can search keywords like "boarding," "dogs," and "stress" to learn as much as possible. Then let this information direct how you move forward when you need to travel.

Most kennels, *especially* the bigger ones that take in hundreds of dogs and cats, are nightmares. It's a huge money-making operation with the *possibility* of very little care being given to your dog. They may have decent intentions, but making money is the biggest one.

The combination of large numbers of animals in the facility and a low number of caring staff or overworked staff increase the probability that your dog will be lonely and ignored. You may have to pay extra to have your dog enjoy the "offered but not included" group play. You may opt out of that because it's only for a short time and you are on a budget, but this could mean that your dog is all alone for *many* hours and may have to resort to peeing/pooping in his or her confined area or, God forbid, a cage.

The noise alone in these places can be enough to stress your dog out. If your dog came from an original situation of abuse or neglect, this type of stress can trigger them. Remember, they do not know that you are coming back (even if you told them repeatedly), so the range of emotions they experience can be intensely damaging, possibly halting whatever progress you have made with them.

When a dog is emotionally triggered, it can set back all the training and hard work you've invested in them, the relationship, and there may even be new fear-based habits that you will have to contend with. No one will know your dog better than you, *no one*, and you will inherently know if boarding should be avoided.

All three of my dogs are way too sensitive for this experience! I tried it. I was at the time new to the state of North Carolina, hence no friends or loved ones to entrust them with, and I traveled to go and see my dad and his wife in Charlotte. It was Thanksgiving, and they would have gladly received me with my loving trio of dogs, but they had a badass Maine Coon cat who not only hated dogs but also hated people that smelled of dogs. I was once attacked by this cat during a prior visit, and so that was my reason for boarding.

I was really in a pickle, and I rationalized that it was only for thirty-six hours. So, being stuck in this situation, I boarded my three dogs together in one of these large boarding facilities, and it was definitely a bad decision. Here's why:

When I got there to pick them up, all of them were brought to me, *and all three dogs pooped in the main check out area*. Excuse me, but what? My heart broke on the spot. I knew their elimination schedules and systems after so many years, and to me this public pooping was due to the *blatant* fact they had *never once* been taken out of their little room. They seemed nervous and hyper, and it was very unsettling, so that was the first and last time I ever boarded them. Yes, I confronted the staff, and yes, they even cut the bill in half (a big surprise), but that very act also told me that they must have known. They knew that for all thirty-six hours my beautiful dogs never once were taken to pee or poop.

Now, I don't assume that every place is run like this, and this could have been an anomaly; I can give them that, but the point in airing this sad event is this: Between the abandonment dogs feel, the risk of kennel cough, and the fact that many dogs feel intense separation anxiety, why not try the alternative?

The Alternative (What is it, you ask?)

Having a dog makes a person more social. Between the dog run, the park, social meet-ups for outings and hikes, by virtue of the fact that you have a dog, you now know people that you probably would not have known otherwise. These people also have dogs and most likely have the same travel needs, at least occasionally, so be smart and take advantage of this potential network. Make it a point to create a list of people and their dogs, with phone numbers and email addresses with the hopes that when people in this group travel, all dogs belonging to this group are cared for by people in the group. For people with multiple dogs, it is a tad more challenging, but I have found that if dogs are well behaved, people will take two.

This is a beautiful method for:

1. Eradicating the possibility of kennel cough (which is awful). Kennel cough is an all-encompassing term used to describe a multitude of highly contagious respiratory illnesses. The real term for it is *Bordetella bronchiseptica*.
2. Your dog will not feel abandoned by you, because he or she will be in the company of their park friends or PAC (playfully active canine) friends. Hence, *zero* anxiety!
3. You will not worry about your furry family member, because you know that they are being cared for by a person that is familiar to them, and that they will be going to a familiar place for a fun outing.
4. It's *free!* It's a barter!

I know that people travel a lot for work (yes, less since COVID), and this specific type of networking gives them the ability to have a dog. People know that dogs are happier and calmer when with others (be it people, dogs, or both). So, for example, with the group I started in NYC all those years ago, people would compare schedules and basically even dog share some days of the week (saving money on dog walking). *Again, it's a barter.* It's a great way of freeing one up, so a busy person doesn't have to run home to "do" their dog quickly and then run out again. It's a lovely and convenient option.

Several decades ago, I boarded my original dog love, Bogie, only one time, and he got kennel cough. It was a miserable experience. It also broke my heart. He even had the Bordetella vaccine, and it was then that I came to discover that it is *not* guaranteed to work (imagine that!). So, after that, I went to the dog run on the weekend in Riverside Park (NYC) and shared this very idea with people. I arrived with a clipboard, and wouldn't you know it? People *loved* the idea! I had a whole list at the end of the several hours I spent focused on doing this in the park. I felt like the mayor, and it paid off! The idea was well received and fully executed. It even evolved to where people made copies of each other's keys and would call one another to arrange spontaneous dog outings as they had events pop up. (Note: this may be more of a city thing).

I am not saying it must go this far, but imagine the freedom to call and arrange with a friend/dog friend once you have the dates for your trip. You simply put it out there, and before you know it, someone, some nice person with a dog your dog is familiar with, says, "Yes, I will take him/her." Then all you do is owe them the same! It's wonderful, it works, and it's free!

Kennels seem to work better for less emotionally needy dogs. Dogs that are wired for sound can benefit from what could turn out to be even more exercise than they are used to in their regular life. This is what a good and well-run kennel has to offer. Note that you can usually watch your dog from your vacation or wherever you are online from their webcam to see how they are faring. Most pet businesses are set up with this fun feature.

Another option is to hire a dog walker/sitter to come three times a day and to just keep your dog in their known environment. This can get extremely pricey, and your dog may still be alone throughout the night. The good news is that these sitters can water plants, take in mail, and feed the cat (and may charge extra), but it may be worth the extra money if your dog doesn't mind being alone at night. Inquire about the different prices, especially for full-on house sitter vs. a three-walk-a-day-plus-feed. It probably makes sense to hire a house sitter.

So, now you have top quality reasons on why and how to avoid boarding, and to make sure that if you must, to choose the right one. Humans tend to be extra trusting when in need, so please take your time and do your homework.

CHAPTER 15

No-Agenda Romps: Walking and Sniffing in Wonder

IT'S JUST NOT FAIR FOR the dog that waits home all day for his or her outside time, for that walk, run, or trip to the dog park to be rushed. There are ton of reasons to be in a rush (a little less during the time of COVID and beyond), but just don't be in a hurry or disconnected—or worse, both—when out with your dog. *This is their time. Honor them by being present!*

I think of the jogging moms and dads wearing earbuds as they get their jog on while pushing the stroller. I've seen kids crying as their parent jogs on, and once I had to stop a mom to let her know that her kid's arm was dangling dangerously outside of the stroller. I'm sure these little babes sense the emotional absence (and joggers, please don't get mad). Therefore, I am sure that dogs can sense this too.

A dog's time out in the world is so limited, so it is a true disappointment to them when you are not fully present, and indeed, you miss out as well. You may be reading this and thinking, "That's nuts, man. Come on, the dog is out. Is that not enough?" Well, maybe for some dogs, like dogs that are super hyper, ball-focused, and high-strung. This type of dog just might not notice your earbuds and can require much less personal attention and emotional connectivity. You may even be able to listen to music, take a call, or play one of the myriad games we are globally addicted to as you throw balls, Frisbees, or sticks for your Type-A dog.

The dogs I would describe as more soulful, well, they may just require extra emotional tending to. You know what I mean? These are the dogs whose feelings run very deep, the dogs that always have eye contact—soul contact, even. These dogs will even follow you into the bathroom or just about everywhere. These are the dogs I am referring to. They love walking next to you on the leash or off, and they still occasionally glance at you to connect. These dogs could be considered needy, but it's because they come from unknown circumstances, and many things and noises (and vacuums) scare the hell out of them. I do find myself catering to it, being a dog mama and all.

So, *just be present,* because not only do dogs crave the great outdoors (be it on leash, running freely, or at the dog run), this is their time with you, and they really cherish it. This is what they dream about from the couch or their fluffy bed or the cold, hard floor (many dogs' preference). It is this time that enables them to be at home for so long, or for any length of time, really. Their outside time is their time to shine, when they get to enjoy some "me" time, just walking or trotting on leash or at their own pace off leash, taking in the scents on the trails, in the woods, and what the city streets have to offer. If only we were as easy to satisfy!

I have always had multiple dogs, and they are usually off leash, running and dashing about, literally with little doggie smiles on their beautiful faces. We simply need to use dog time to relax while we walk them, walking *with* them, at their pace. Walk with them in wonder—in wonder of them and nature. They surely enjoy nature. Let us take this cue from them. Since everything else is on our schedule and pace, this is really an opportunity for us to slow down and simply be with our magical dogs. Enough with the phones already!

There is so much we can learn from being present and observing them. They alternate from running to jogging and back to walking, sometimes stopping for *very* long periods to sniff at seemingly nothing. However, it's never nothing; it is something very wonderous to them, and sniff they must! Their intricate nose and keen sensory system make a regular walk a godly adventure. They are just ecstatic to be alive and on this walk.

When truly present, we bear witness to their joy as we bask in our mutual love.

Have a love affair with your dog!

CHAPTER 16

PAC Play and Dog Walkers That Hike

THE IMPORTANCE OF YOUR DOG having dog friends cannot be stressed enough. Whatever you think, or feel, or fear, you *must* make sure that you socialize your dog from the get-go, unless you take on a challenging adoptee that simply cannot be around other dogs.

Dogs are PAC animals and truly enjoy the company of other dogs. I always felt awful for the dog attached to a chain in the yard—a "guard dog." So sad! All they want is love, exercise, good food, and a real connection with their person.

Try to make an effort, because hanging out with other dogs satisfies a primal need in your dog. They love to play, play fight, and compete for toys. They love running as fast as they can (sometimes in circles). They play games you'll never understand, they hump one another (*not* sexual, yet humans get so upset!), gang up on others, and it's all an absolute riot—*if you are not uptight* and have faith in your dog.

If you believe your dog is unfriendly (possibly due to misperceived growling and snarling behavior), and you then keep him or her isolated from other dogs, the more you deprive your dog and the more you remove their God-given instinct to have companions. The real issue here is that people misperceive their dog's behavior a *very* large percentage of the time. If they see a dog lift a lip, they may think their dog is vicious and then isolate their dog for its life, out of their own fear.

I have seen this a lot! I have even asked a few fearful dog owners to trust me and allow me to take said isolated dog on an adventure with the PAC. When given the chance, and not in the presence of their nervous and fearful owner, these dogs played very well with the others, and they were able to shine!

Dogs only have so many noises and expressions, and many of them are misunderstood. They then get classified as bad or unfriendly or "hates other dogs," thus sadly never being allowed to properly socialize.

I Am Being Repetitive Purposefully!

The truth is that when your dog gets to be active and playful on a regular basis, the healthier and more fit their bodies and minds become. Again, kind of like us humans!

A short, simple walk around the block daily does *not* suffice. Dogs need to experience some freedom and adventure to keep their senses alive. They need to run as fast as they can because they release endorphins as we do when we run, so it's good for their overall sense of well-being. It is so important to afford them their joy. They probably have to lay around much of the day so these adventures are literally good for everything.

So, if you work a regular job and your best friend is home all day, kindly remember that unless your dog is very old, or sick, or just gave birth, they need you to make sure that they get out and get their dog on, *doggone it!*

There are dog walkers now that hike. These types of dog walkers are popping up all over the country—you just need to find one in your area. If you have a regular dog walker, why not suggest that he or she take two or three of their dog "jobs" out together to an enclosed dog run? Maybe a long, one-hour walk in the woods? Let them know if your dog is okay off leash.

Start That Conversation

If a dog walker charges, let's say, $15 per half hour walk, it's about three hours for them, with driving, to accomplish four dog walks. If there are three dogs on a one-hour walk/hike together, that is $60. It's better money, less time, and a much better time for the dogs. The dog walker makes good money doing something they love, and this style gives them more time to make more money and make even more dogs happy! It all makes good sense, and it's all to the dog's benefit.

If you knew that your dog would be out for a few hours right in the middle of your workday, picked up at noon and returned by two o'clock, that would be great, right? Your dog would be quick to get in that habit of the "basics" walk in the morning and happily wait four hours for their big daily adventure. During this time, they have social interaction with dogs that will become their friends (dogs really do have friends). They will have exercise, and they will experience new freedom. This gains them doggie autonomy, and that is a *very* good thing.

Some dog walkers have caught on to the money that can be made but are not *true* dog lovers. Try to weed these people out! If they are in it solely for the dough, they will cut corners by cutting time short (not likely your dog can complain about it), they will *not* be fully present, and they will not create an experience that is of maximum enjoyment for your dog. These are the people on their phone the whole time or listening to music. I am not saying that that is a high crime, and yes, I did both from time to time when I had my business, but I am referring to the person who is never *not* on their devices, and your dog deserves better than that.

Ask them these questions:

- Are you a dog lover?
- Do you wear headphones while with my dog?
- Do they always get the full half-hour or full hour?
- Always?
- Do you have a dog?
- Tell me about your dog.
- Tell me about how much you love dogs.

Whoever you are speaking with has the chance to prove their authenticity, and you need to observe it. Don't hire someone who decided to do this solely for the money. You could regret it. Hire a person that has soul and true love and compassion for animals.

Know What to Look For, and Look For It

The expense of this type of service is just another life expense. These beautiful creatures are not cheap to have. Dogs are *not* a hobby. Dogs require good food and exercise, so never feel guilty about spending this money, as it is your duty. I used to spend $400 a month on a dog walker (before I became one) and would always imagine that money in the bank or what it could buy. I didn't do this with the electric or water bills. I didn't imagine money piling up if I didn't pay my car insurance. I had to shift the paradigm, change my perspective.

When I had my business, Dog Day Afternoon, there were certainly people that couldn't afford my services daily. There were the Tuesday/Thursday people and the M/W/F people, and

I respected their choices. I would sometimes lower my prices for their needs, which I never regretted, because once I got to know each dog and they became my friend, I wanted to get them out more. Therefore, my little homemade business thrived the way it did for eight years. I considered all my PAC members my friends. I respected each soul and knew what they needed.

You want a woke dog walker!

CHAPTER 17

Not Everyone Wants to Make Out With a Dog

THERE ARE PEOPLE WHO REALLY want to be animal people, but may struggle with this, wondering why it might not be so innate for them. They may compare themselves with their friends or perhaps people they have merely witnessed. People that sleep with their dog(s), share ice cream cones sloppily, and even mouth kiss. They may worry that they are not in this category of dog people. They may even be grossed out a bit by them.

Not everyone wishes to share their bed with a four legged creature, but it does not mean that they are not dog people. It does not mean that they are uptight (well some may be), or missing that dog-loving gene.

So what? There is no right or wrong. We can all manage to have cats and dogs and love them precisely just the way that we do. We all don't have four animals or more and make them the absolute center of the universe. For some of us, it is hard not to, but it is *absolutely not required*, as long as the creatures we do have are loved and cared for properly.

There are animals and pet situations of *all* kinds.

Lisa Andrea Snyder

CHAPTER 18

Sleeping With Dogs

THIS IS USUALLY DIFFERENT FOR men and women. I try to avoid generalizing, but after conversations with so many women who have told me that their husbands/boyfriends are absolute in their opinion of the subject, I am forced to have this observation (but naturally there are exceptions).

With the new dog owner in mind, this issue will come up. If you adopt/buy or in any way acquire a dog, you may in the beginning utilize a crate. Crates and crate training can be great for puppies and for dogs that have known trauma. Crates are always used as a safe space and never used for punishment. A crate should be a place of comfort for your dog.

Once past this phase, the issue may arise of where the dog will sleep.

Knowing that a dog has four paws, may have stepped in shite, been in the dirt/mud, etc., it is an obvious choice that the answer could or should be a resolute *not in my/our bed*. So, I want to speak up strongly on this topic. While dogs can step in a variety of substances during their day, they typically have a strong desire to share your bed. We have all seen the funny posts of dogs overtaking their human's bed, with people having a sliver of space compared to their stretched-out dog(s). It does *not* have to be like that. Your dog(s) will be so happy to be allowed to sleep with you that they will lie where and how you allow them to. It just takes a little repetition and patience.

I am sorry to say that if you have a Chihuahua or several other types of smalls, you are plumb out of luck. It is your absolute duty and responsibility to allow them to burrow. Several types of dogs are listed as burrowers, including Dachshunds, Cairn terriers, Schnauzers, and even Siberian huskies (but especially the Chihuahua). While a husky may be difficult to accommodate, the littler dogs are super easy. You can also fake them out by covering them with a throw on the top of your bed. My dog Luke is not so easily fooled, and no matter how hard I try, he ends up right next to me, skin to fur by the morning.

Whatever this may mean to them, why be so resolute in denying them? I assure you it is not a power move; they are not trying to dominate you, and it is not your job to put them in their place. Mankind has dominion over all/most animals. You do not have to prove you are the alpha (you are!). Just allow this time to be the time of comfort for you, or the two of you, and enjoy it.

In order to get your harder-to-convince bedmate to agree (or even to try it), simply make sure you do a wipe down of all the paws. (Having three dogs and being a neat freak, I got used to, *very* early on, cleaning all twelve paws upon entering my home.) If your dog has extremely curly hair or fur, brush them regularly. This is good to do anyway, as there are many things you may discover, like they are losing their coat or they have a patch of dried mud, sap, or something else from rolling on the ground.

At the height of my dog and cat family, I woke up with three dogs and a cat on my head (sharing a pillow). I could even get up and make coffee and crawl back into bed with them all.

I consider this time a precious time. Bea stopped sleeping with me altogether (she much preferred a cold floor and to be by the front door). Protector dogs can be like that. They sleep with you because they know *you* want to and need to, but then as soon as you are "down," off they go to protect.

Currently, I only sleep with two dogs, one that burrows and one that sleeps on top at my feet.

I make sure I clean my sheets each week, as opposed to . . . well, I guess I used to clean sheets much less, and never have I ever been grossed out or surprised by anything. Dogs do not poop or pee on your bed (dogs and people both do not do this, thankfully), and if they were to do that, well, this is definitely *not* a dog to sleep

with, and so please get to the bottom of that—it could be something medical.

There is one exception, and that is if they've been exposed to poison ivy, poison oak, or poison sumac (sumac being more allergenic than the other two). If you have a backyard and have any of these growing or are a constant woods explorer/hiker, you may be protected mostly by your clothes, but your dog can very easily brush up against these plants. Dogs are mostly spared (it is extremely rare they experience actual symptoms) due to the oils being blocked by their fur, but both cats and dogs can be carriers of the oils, which can then be transmitted to their beloved humans.

The poisons are a *very* good reason to curb your sleeping habits during the time that they are prevalent. This will vary depending on where you live. Also, be careful with cats especially, because we tend to pick them up like little babies, and that for me has proven unfortunate many times.

If you (or your kids) do get a case of poison ivy, oak, or sumac, I have found rubbing alcohol to be tremendously beneficial initially, and then a product called Ivarest. I have had some really bad cases of poison "stuff," and this is an excellent product. It's very similar to calamine lotion, but better. There are also other measures to take, such as bathing your pet *as soon as possible*, but please wear rubber gloves while you do this. (Also wear clothing that blocks contact with your pet, and throw them in the wash when finished.)

During this bath, use plenty of pet shampoo (or Dawn—the ultimate degreaser). Create a nice foamy lather, and make sure you cover all parts of their coat. Please be super careful to avoid their ears, eyes, and, I have heard, genitals.

Rinse them *a lot*. Rinse them thoroughly. The best part is how happy they are when it is over. They love to be dried, and post-bath time is always a great opportunity to gently check in on their ears and clean them. Just make sure they do not run outside directly to where those pesky plants could be. You can also have a professional landscaper or arborist come and see just what you have growing on your property and remove it.

To conclude, we spend a third of our lives sleeping—and cats and dogs spend more. Why be separate? If you clean your sheets, launder your blankets regularly, and check them for anything that could be gross, dogs are the perfect bedfellows. Some love to cuddle; some can even spoon (don't judge me). Some love to have their head on a pillow. If you can allow for this type of contact and connection, I assure you that you will be richer for it.

Regarding kids, it's a natural to have them sleep together, and you might even find it easier to put your kid to bed with the dog. Just make sure they have *both* peed before bedtime.

P.S.—Dogs know it's special and that they are lucky if they are allowed!

CHAPTER 19

The Sweetness of an Old Dog

MOST DOGS HAVE A SWEETNESS about them that is undeniable. I say most because mean dogs certainly exist, but there is usually a reason for it. Usually, they were not treated so well—possibly neglected or abused or both. Dogs, whatever their disposition may be naturally, tend to acquire an even sweeter one as they age. It's like the grumpy old man who mellows with age and becomes super sweet (my own dad, for one, but we all know *that* guy). It must be something about the aging process.

If you are lucky enough to have a dog for many years, you will notice this. If it's possible, old, sweet dogs will make you love them even more. You will see the age on their faces, a greying outline on their ears, and their eyes may become cloudy. You will feel such an abundance of love for them, even more than you do now.

You will notice them moving about more carefully, so be sure to adjust your handling of them. They may not be able to rough play or fetch the way they did. Frisbee may be completely off the table. They may not run so much anymore, or at all. There may be a new look in their eyes, a look that might also be asking you to slow down, so please take a moment to feel these new needs and respond accordingly. You will want to limit their exercise because their heart and lung function deteriorates with age, and you will see by the way that they move their bodies what could possibly be ailing them (read the chapter on the power of massage).

There are many ways to update and improve the way(s) that you take care of your aging canine, from food (switching to lower proteins as they get harder to digest) to being aware they are more sensitive to extreme temperature changes due to a shift in their metabolism.

I highly recommend dog lovers get the book, "Good Old Dog: Expert Advice For Keeping Your Aging Dog Happy, Healthy, And Comfortable," written by Nicholas Dodman, for it really is a treasure.

We all come to realize just how temporary our dogs' lives are. All our lives are temporary, but at least humans have the potential to live up to 100 years and even more. We all wish dogs got even a quarter of those possible human years. Therefore, we must make the most of the years they do have by loving them, spending good solid time with them, and creating as many adventures and memories as possible.

I use the word "adventure" a lot. We *all* need adventures, and without them life is flat. For a dog, a basic walk is an adventure. They are so easy to please, so anything above and beyond a basic walk is a true gift to them.

Give that gift and give it freely. It will only benefit you and your family. Look into your dogs' eyes and speak softly and kindly to them. They are here for you every step of the way. When the world is unkind and you have a bad day, your dog's kindness can see you through. Our dogs make us better people. They make our lives richer and sweeter.

Speaking about our senior dog population, the shelters are absolutely filled with them. Most of them spend the rest of their days there and were usually brought into these shelters when their owner died. If it is a kill shelter, imagine a dog being loved and revered one day and brought to a loud, scary shelter the next (when all the relatives turned a blind eye). I am not saying this to make you sad, I am merely suggesting that you consider adopting a senior. They are calm, they have had a lot of life experience, and they still have love to offer. They are happy to be there for you, just for less time, and they almost always come trained. Adoption of a senior dog is one of the most noble acts a human dog lover can carry out.

A shout out for senior cats too!

As I write this chapter, I glance over at my beautiful dog Bea. I have been with her since she was six months old in 2007. I know that we are on borrowed time. I cry when I think of what her life and loyalty have meant to me in all these years, and I cannot imagine my life without her by my side. Bea has put up with my fostering and adopting multiple dogs. She has been there to break up arguments with other dogs and people. She is warm, kind, and intuitive. She is bonded to my nieces, Grace and Ava, and loves them deeply.

Bea never ever has been wrong about anyone, and I love her more than I can say. There are not even words. I hope that by the time this book is published she is still with me so she can see her nose on the cover.

Some people do not get a dog because of their fear of this type of loss. We have *all* met that person who had a dog and will never again go through that. Right? It's just too hard. I disagree, and I address this very sentiment in the next chapter, "Letting Go." (Read the poem!)

To sum up, dogs are sweet, but this sweetness inexplicably multiplies as they become old. This sweetness calls for us to love them even more, which comes easily and naturally, and it makes sure we keep up with their needs.

I urge anyone who works from home and may want a dog, but not a puppy so much, to please consider a dog that is older.

Lastly is the example of my sixteen-year-old-plus Portuguese water dog, Mia. When I had Dog Day Afternoon, one of my clients died, leaving nine-year-old Mia all alone. I fostered her until the family figured out what they were going to do (they were *not* dog people). Long story short, I kept her. She was so vibrant at nine and lived for another healthy seven years. Mia was the perfect example of a happy dog. Her prior person loved her so, and I kept the tradition going, and Mia thrived. I kept waiting for her to get old, but she simply refused. Until she didn't. Her good genes and vitality were revelatory. People would comment on the blackness and shine of her coat. When I would tell people she was sixteen, the reply was usually that of shock.

I fed her well, she got plenty of exercise (oh, my God, this breed needs it), and we loved her. Oh, how we loved our Measle Weasel, and she *felt* that love and lived a good, long life. Mia also loved toast—Turkish toast with Irish butter. When Mia died, she did so after her last piece of toast.

Oh, Mia, thank you for all those years.

My point is that the adoption of a dog that is seven, eight, nine, or even ten and older, if you step up and give that senior an amazing life, they may just surprise you. Do not assume an older dog means illness and vet bills; that is possible at any age.

Something to consider!

CHAPTER 20

Letting Go: The Best Poem Ever and Dealing With The Death Of Your Dog

DOGS DIE. THEY DO NOT live nearly long enough, yet this is no reason not to get a dog. It's certainly not a reason not to get *another* dog.

People truly suffer after their beloved dog dies, and for many the result of such pain and loss comes the decision never to get another dog, to never feel such sadness ever again.

The poem I am about to share with you really clarifies this deep emotional reaction. *We are all going to die.* All of us and our animals, our kids, their kids, *all of us*. So, we must *celebrate the temporary* (as the Buddhist practice tells us).

Here is my favorite piece of writing on the subject, and it perfectly conveys the premise of this little book.

The Love I Left Behind

Before humans die, they write their last will and testament, giving their home and all they have to those they leave behind. If, with my paws, I could do the same, this is what I'd ask . . .

To a poor and lonely stray, I'd give:
—My happy home
—My bowl and cozy bed, soft pillows and all my toys
—The lap, which I loved so much

90

—The hand that stroked my fur and the sweet voice that spoke my name.

I'd will to the sad, scared shelter dog the place I had in my human's loving heart, of which there seemed no bounds.

So, when I die, please do not say, "I will never have a pet again, for the loss and the pain is more than I can stand."

Instead, go find an unloved dog, one whose life has held no joy or hope and give my place to him.

—Author Unknown

This piece of literature simply and beautifully says it all. Are you in tears? I am.

As I near the end of writing this little book, my dog Bea lays by my side. Her eyes are cloudy, and sometimes I fear her breathing is too fast, but the vet says she is fine. She walks slower and more carefully now, and she holds her gaze when our eyes lock. Is she trying to tell me something? When she goes to lay down, she does it ever so slowly, as if the stiffness overtakes her, and I pray she is not in pain. I do not think she is.

I know that at fifteen-plus, her days on the planet are limited.

I give her a supplement for arthritis, and for about four years she has been on a prescription drug for bladder control. She had had a few small accidents, but none since she's been on it. It builds up the lining of the bladder wall, and it works. Bea is still play fighting with Max the cat, and she still goes on each romp outdoors, only now we are all accustomed to walking at her slower pace. She is still indulging her intense and natural need to sniff incessantly and I take that as a very good sign.

So, become more patient. Know how fleeting these days are in the end years, and love every second. So far, my Bea is okay, but I know how this goes, as I have been here before.

We must know and accept their temporary stay the day that you bring your puppy or dog home. Accept your dog's aging and your dog's death with grace. Be grateful for the years of love your dog gave to you so freely and mourn. Don't mourn too long or say that you can *never* do this again or that it's just too hard. A true dog person, the truest dog lover, understands that this day will come, hopefully in many, *many* years. This dog lover knows that it is their duty to heal and get out there again, because there are always dogs in need.

Do not use the death of your dog to quash future dog companionship.

Take the time that is right for you to grieve, but stay tuned in. Somehow, if you let yourself be guided, the spirit of your old dog will whisper in your ear, "It's time." Don't let the pain of grieving diminish a chance to bond with another. Keep that heart of yours open. It is not easy, but you can do it, and imagine/know that you are being guided by your dog's spirit (your spirit dog).

You know the dog I speak of, and they would not want you to be alone.

CHAPTER 21

Oh, One Last Thing . . . Choosing Dogs

AS A PERSON WHO DECIDED early on not to get married or have children, I have been told over the years that maybe (*just* maybe), if I hadn't had so many dogs, two usually, once four and currently three, that perhaps I would have. My grandmother was the first one to suggest such a concept when I tipped the scales with two dogs in my early thirties, and over the years, a sister and other friends have rung that bell. I never cared or reacted because that's just how it is in our society.

I might have compensated for many a lack with dogs, or perhaps I misplaced my love and focused on the wrong species? Who knows? Who cares? All I do know is that I have no regrets. I think I simply *chose* dogs.

I chose dogs because of who they are and how that love added to and changed my life for the better. I chose dogs because I always feel kind and gentle and the very best version of myself when in their midst. I did not choose dogs over people, over a mate, or over kids. I chose dogs for who *they* are and how much happiness they bring me.

Practically everyone has children, right? They are a biological force, and this force seriously makes its way into a person's life, planned or not. If you do not have a child, well, something just might be wrong with you, and people really do not know what to make of you, particularly if you're a woman that does not procreate. It's 2022, and this world still doesn't know what to fully make of a woman on her own. I guess I am a modern-day spinster, a dog lady, a cat lady, an animal freak, but . . . if I were a man, I'd just be a cool bachelor.

Ruff ruff!

So, I hereby dedicate this lil' book to my beautiful animals and to those of you who, by choice or even inadvertently, chose dogs *just because*. I look at this world a little unconventionally, and if you do too, I want to validate you.

Most of our parents want grandchildren, not granddogs. Of course, they will take both, but just a granddog, not so much.

I want to state for thee ole record, "Psssst, it's okay!"

To have a child is the ultimate sacrifice, truly. I admit that it is probably the most incredibly rewarding act a human can do. It is noble, it is huge, and I *always* knew that.

Through friends that decided that their twenties was a good time to have a child, or multiple children, I saw that most of the heavy lifting fell on the shoulders of women. Don't get pissed off, great daddies out there, I said mostly.

I decided to wait. The more I waited, the more my life took root. I waited some more and saw more friends struggle. I might not have known exactly what I wanted, but I sure did know what I did *not* want. I came from a dysfunctional family filled with alcoholism, addiction, sarcasm, and narcissism. I simply could *not* bear to imagine being at the helm of a noisy, active, food-needing family, so I guess I literally took a hard pass. I never met "the one" anyway, and so I just proceeded to create a life packed with friends, career (jobs), travel, and social life.

When I was in my twenties, I did, however, fall madly in love with my first dog in Los Angeles. Bogie was adopted by my neighbor (a private chef for actor Steven Seagal), and this woman mostly kept him in her yard in the Hollywood Hills, along with her giant rottweiler, Odetta. Odetta was a huge and splendid specimen who did not care to share her space with this young, male, black-and-tan mixed breed, and he was able to escape the yard (because he was brilliant and just skinny enough to get through the fence). Up to that point, I had never had a dog, only cats. I adopted Bogie from this chef, and this relationship went on to develop superbly—the depth of our bond was magical. The nobility Bogie exhibited was stupendous, and it was the beginning of my infatuation with the dog species.

I knew and even declared out loud that if I never became a parent to a human child that it would be perfectly fine, that just having and loving a dog would perfectly suffice for me. *Note: I am a very caring woman, very loving and maternal. That has not gone wasted.* For some people, there is no choice but to have children. I utterly respect that. I get it. I felt that parenthood was such a huge topic, and I really thought about it. I have no regrets—*none*.

I am happy and grateful for my sister though. She stepped up to the plate and had two wonderful daughters. I love you, Grace! I love you, Ava!

I worry about them, and I think about them all of the time, and I do think that *not* having kids of my own was a very good call. I say this with self-awareness, self-love, and compassion. I think I would have been a helicopter parent, overly involved, overly concerned, and no kid wants that.

Dogs and cats, friends, and hosting dinners in my home has been extraordinarily rewarding, as I am a person that needs and seeks peace.

So, you do you, however you see fit. Just remember . . . there will always be a dog that needs you and loves you.

Thank you so very much for reading this book. Thank you from the bottom of my heart.

THE DEATH OF MY DOG BEA

ON MAY 25, 2022, MY best girl, Bea, the soulmate of my lifetime, left her body and entered the unlimited realm, the sky, heaven, etc. She was exactly fifteen years and three months old. The night before, she went for a long walk along the Hudson River (at The Hook Trail along the Hudson River in Nyack NY), had her favorite meal, and was in a great mood. Bea was a big fan of dinner, sitting so patiently while I prepared it. Bea would bark and act playful, and lovingly attack our cat Max, who was also waiting for his meal. Sometimes she would bark relentlessly, which I always found funny because she rarely barked. I guess just the thought of her special dinners made her super happy and frisky. This ritual went on for over fifteen years.

Later that evening, she didn't want to come outside for the before-bed pee, which I did take note of, and then, during the night, I heard her make those chirpy dream sounds, and they were kind of loud. I didn't think much of it, but I regret not checking on her and laying with her. At 6 a.m. I awoke to that same noise and went in to see her. Bea had wedged herself between the wall and the sofa, a place I had never seen her, and in my heart *I knew*. Her paws were oddly splayed outward and I immediately called Dr. Laura, my trusted veterinarian and friend.

Bea was alive until 9:30 a.m. I had to make a fast decision to end her life. I could have raced over to a different facility (as my vet no longer did surgeries) and run a panel of tests to find out exactly what was going on … have a blood transfusion, but … I did not, because … I knew.

What I knew in my heart and soul was the profound truth that Bea had walked her last walk and had eaten her last meal. For God's sake, she could not stand! How did my best girl go from running and silliness the night before to not being able to stand overnight?

96

Dr. Laura said it was a ruptured tumor. She had seen it hundreds of times before and even her own dog Bo had succumbed to it. Dogs can have tumors that go unnoticed, and then they rupture, and the resulting effects can be devastating. Death can also occur.

I thought of it as Bea being profoundly considerate. There was no drama (well, besides the obvious), she didn't suffer, and at fifteen-plus, I had no time to do anything other than make that right decision to let her go. I was surrounded by my family; my two beautiful nieces by my side.

We were together saying goodbye to the best dog in the world, Bea, who had given us all so much.

We were crying and telling her how much we loved her as she left. I thanked her repeatedly for choosing me, and for some reason, I didn't lose it. I was in my deepest grief, but I felt strong.

In those moments, I felt hyper alive and grateful. I wasn't screaming and crying and inconsolable, like with my first dog Bogie, and if I were to guess, God was present.

I knew that Bea had lived her best life, and her life was over. The unimaginable happened. All those years of saying, "I don't know what I'll do without her" … the reality was upon me.

Oddly, I felt a peaceful feeling, that four weeks to the day later, I still feel. I am moving slower, and I know I am grieving; it just doesn't look like I thought it would.

When I think of her, when I feel her, which is a lot, I feel happy. Different memories appear in my mind and my heart swells. I allow them to play out and sometimes I cry and sometimes I talk to her. Sometimes both occur. Mostly I feel a stillness, a stillness that did not exist before my girl left. I am allowing it to take root; I feel richer. I even feel stronger, somehow inspired.

Bea was my soulmate. She was my baby, my little girl, my friend, my partner in all outdoor activity, and then she was my old lady. I watched her morph from one phase to the next with quiet nobility. Bea had class. She was wise, she was kind, and she had a great sense of humor.

Bea died the day after the Uvalde, Texas, shootings. She got to live to be over fifteen. Those kids did not, so it was all in perspective. I joined the country in grieving the victims of yet another senseless tragedy while I also grieved my dog. Within a few days, I was still in shock and feeling grief for all those kids and teachers and all the extended families that were forever changed on that day, but I began feeling happy about Bea. Thoughts of her were a comfort and I simply felt happy that she was my dog for so long, and grateful that she was who she was.

I felt proud that I did everything I could for those fifteen-plus years to enable and facilitate such a wonderful life for her. I told her good job, and I also told myself the same.

Dog ownership is a friendship, a glorious loving and loyal friendship. There is nothing else like it. When it is your dog's time, simply let go. Be right there with them as they live their last moments. As they draw their last breath, stand strong. It really is a spiritual time. Don't extend their lives with last ditch efforts so that you don't have to say goodbye. They don't need that; they simply need you to be calm and to be with them. We owe them this. They do not fear death like we do. Let him go. Let her go. Celebrate their life, what your life is and was thanks to them.

Fully grieve and then when it is right, your beloved dog will guide you through thoughts, or perhaps a dream. They will let you know precisely when it is okay to get another dog. Therefore, remain open and honor their wishes and give a new dog (or perhaps a new old dog) a home.

Love is energy.

We have so much love to give, and animals need our love. Oh, how we humans need them.

Love and grief. Grief and love are connected and we cannot have one without the other. I will never have another Bea. She was the light when I experienced darkness, and she loved me. I will grieve my loss for a long time, but I will also carry on with gratitude.

When we get a dog, it is the deal we make. We agree that one day, someday far into the future, that we will lose them. We